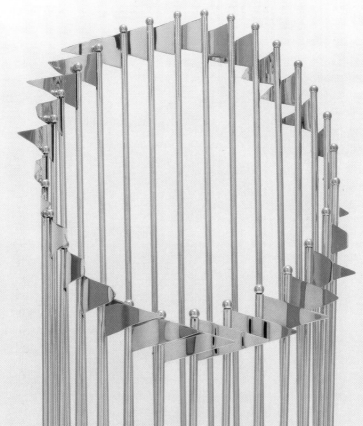

# TWENTY-SEVEN

*The Official Yankees World Series Championship Commemorative*

WORLD SERIES CHAMPIONS

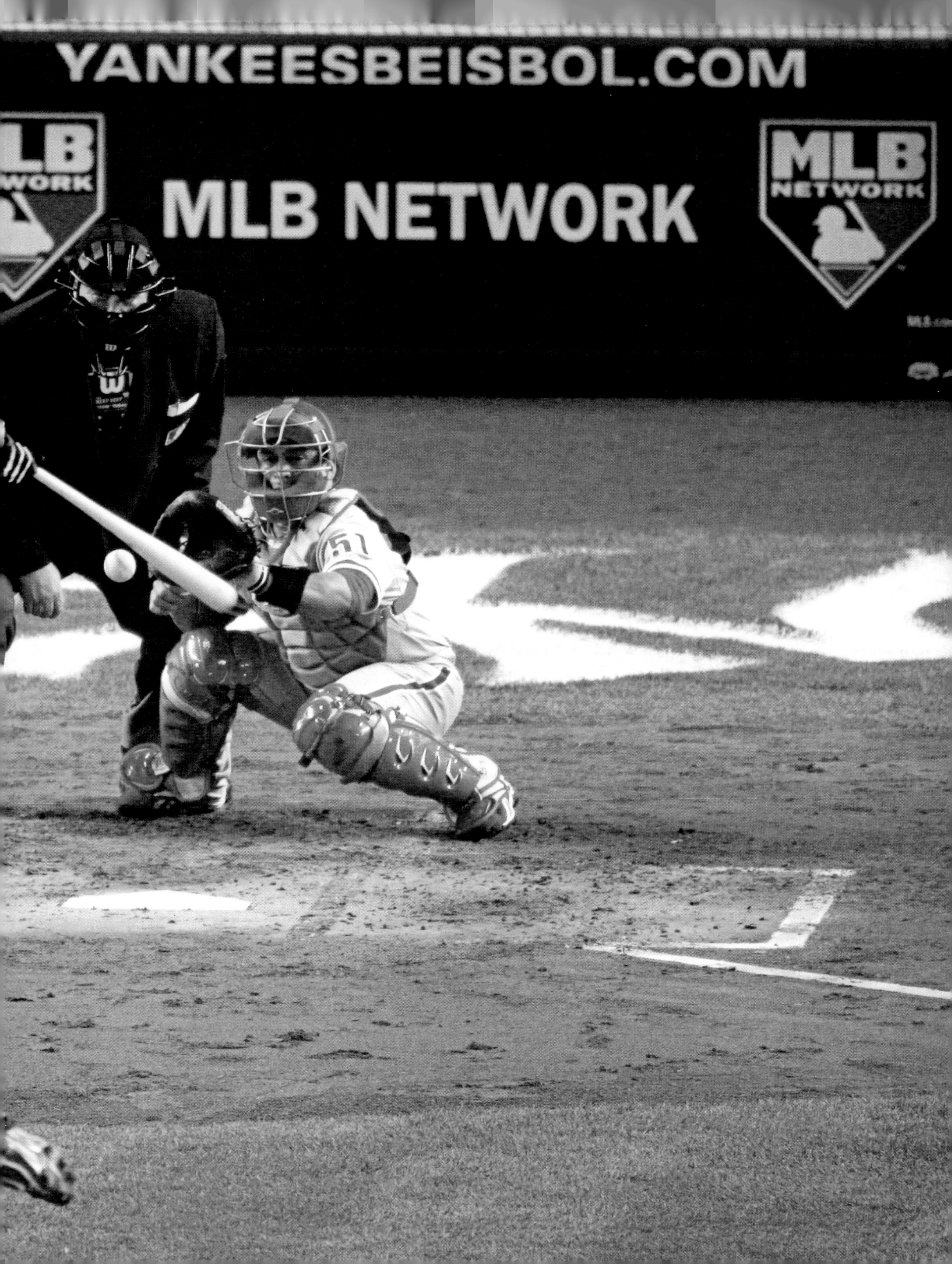
YANKEESBEISBOL.COM
MLB NETWORK
MLB NETWORK
51

RARE AIR BOOKS

A Division of Rare Air Media


**TWENTY-SEVEN**

**The Official Yankees World Series Championship Commemorative**

Created and Produced by Rare Air Books

Designed by Rare Air Media
Printed and bound in the United States

10 9 8 7 6 5 4 3 2 1

Library of Congress Cataloging-in-Publication Data

ISBN-13: 978-0-9820512-4-5
ISBN-10: 0-9820512-4-7

| EDITORS | PHOTOGRAPHERS | DESIGNERS |
|---|---|---|
| Alfred Santasiere III | Ariele Goldman | John Vieceli |
| Mark Vancil | Lou Rocco | Marc L. Miller |
| Ken Derry | James Petrozzello | Matt Jeans |
| Kristina M. Dodge | Linda Cataffo | Andrew Mazurek |
| Nathan Maciborski | Eileen Barroso | Allia Strong |
| Craig Tapper | Getty Images | |

TABLE OF CONTENTS

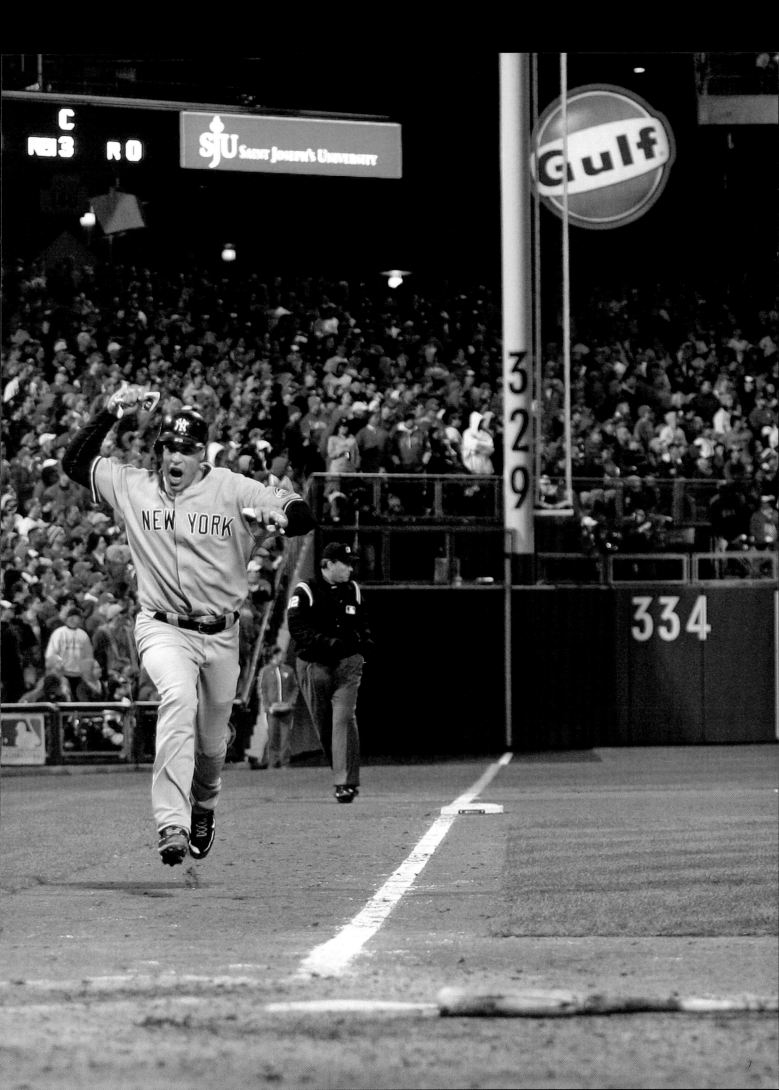

# INTRODUCTION

*When I think about the 2009 New York Yankees, the word that comes to mind is resilience. We started off slowly. We had a lot of disappointment early. But whenever we lost a few games in a row, we took off again. It showed me we had a club that was extremely resilient and a club that was extremely close.*

*There were a few notable signs early on that things were coming together. One was in April, when CC Sabathia pitched so well — even though he lost — in Detroit. That was when he got on a roll. I think the come-from-behind walk-off wins against Minnesota in May were part of the beginning, as well. But it all seemed to change in June with Francisco Cervelli's home run in Atlanta. We took off at that point.*

*But when you lose three in a row in Anaheim right before the All-Star break, how do you come out of that?*

*You know what? We found a way to win, and we cruised. That's not to say it was easy. We talked about staying together and handling adversity the right way. These guys know how to do it and know that it works.*

*When you're with a club that was this enjoyable to manage and you accomplished your goal of winning a world championship, you don't want the season to end. There's joy in the success, but there's also a little sadness because it ends so abruptly.*

*Now, I start thinking about next year and some of the moves we need to make and how to keep this good thing going, but I also go into offseason mode. I go to bed early. I get up early. It's back to being a husband and a daddy. And for me, that's a great celebration.*

*Twenty-Seven is a celebration of accomplishing our goal in 2009 and a celebration of you, the fans. I have said this championship is dedicated to The Boss, Mr. George M. Steinbrenner III, but it's also dedicated to you. So enjoy, and get ready to help us defend the title next season.*

*Joe Girardi*
*Manager*
*New York Yankees*

# SEASON IN REVIEW

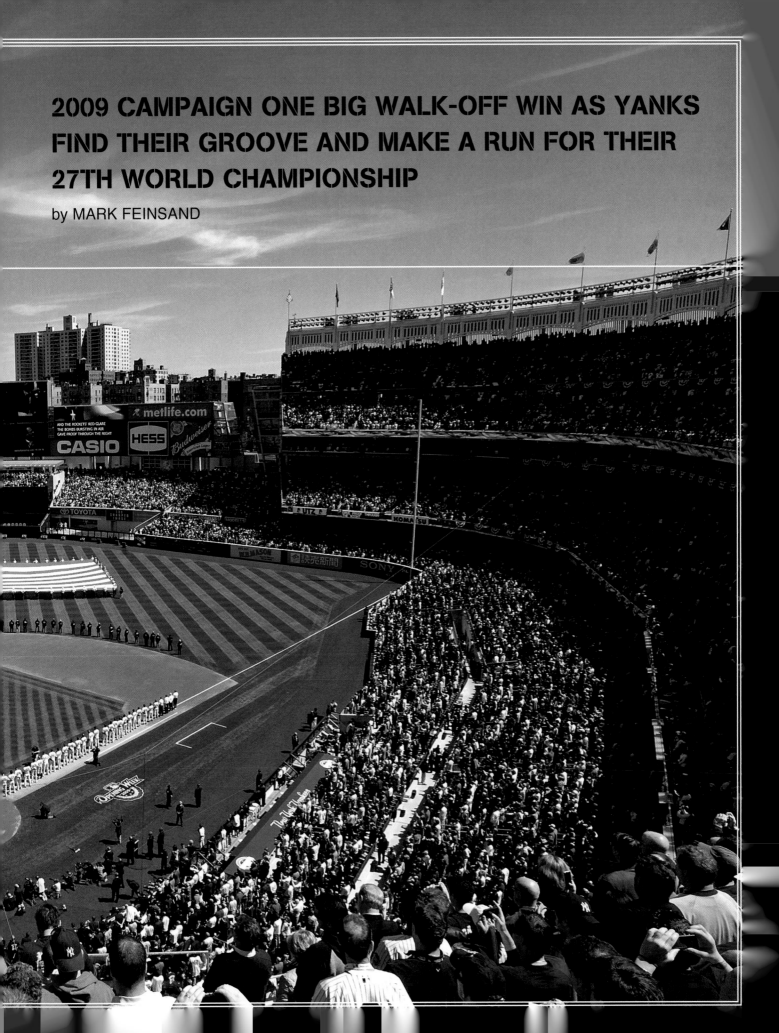

# 2009 CAMPAIGN ONE BIG WALK-OFF WIN AS YANKS FIND THEIR GROOVE AND MAKE A RUN FOR THEIR 27TH WORLD CHAMPIONSHIP

by MARK FEINSAND

# THE YANKEES' RISE BACK TO THE TOP OF THE AMERICAN LEAGUE CAN BE ATTRIBUTED TO THREE THINGS: SUPERB PITCHING, AN EXPLOSIVE OFFENSIVE ATTACK — AND PIES.
## LOTS AND LOTS OF PIES.

POSADA

RODRIGUEZ

After adding three premier free agents to an already impressive roster of talent, the Yankees entered the season with one goal in mind: a return to October.

Mark Teixeira, CC Sabathia and A.J. Burnett helped make that happen in their first year in pinstripes, but it took a lot more than the three newcomers to get the Yankees back to the top of the American League East.

Derek Jeter and Johnny Damon had career-type seasons at the top of the lineup while Alex Rodriguez returned from a difficult spring and March hip surgery to post yet another 30-home run, 100-RBI season. Hideki Matsui reminded everybody what he could do when healthy, and Jorge Posada bounced back from shoulder surgery to reclaim his spot as one of the top offensive catchers in the league.

All in all, the Yankees lineup boasted

"IT WAS A BIG MOMENT, COMING OUT IN THE NEW STADIUM AND LOOKING BACK ... JETER'S THERE AND POSADA IS BEHIND THE PLATE. THAT WILL BE A LASTING MEMORY FOR ME."

—SABATHIA

SABATHIA

"I LOVE SEEING A MANAGER STICK UP FOR HIS TEAM. IT WAS A BAD CALL, AND JOE STOOD UP FOR US. HE KNOWS WE'RE BATTLING OUT THERE, SO HE'S GOING TO GO BATTLE FOR US."

—TEIXEIRA

TEIXEIRA

POSADA

MATSUI

seven players with at least 20 home runs, tying a big-league record, and their 244 home runs set a new franchise mark.

"When we're down by one run, other teams really need to be careful," Damon said. "Anyone in the lineup is capable of hitting one out."

As impressive as the offense was, the pitching staff did its part in leading the Yankees to 103 victories, the most by a Bombers team since 2002. Sabathia tied for the major league lead with 19 wins while Mariano Rivera posted his seventh 40-save season and his ninth with a sub-2.00 ERA.

Even with a slow start to the season, the Yankees had plenty to celebrate in April with the opening of their new baseball cathedral. The team dropped the home opener on April 16, but the loss couldn't mute the significance of the day.

"Just coming out of that bullpen and getting ready for the game, I'll always remember that first time," said Sabathia, who threw the Stadium's first pitch. "It was a big moment, coming out in the new Stadium and looking back … Jeter's there and Posada is behind the plate. That will be a lasting memory for me."

Sabathia's spikes were one of three keepsakes taken by the National Baseball Hall of Fame and Museum, which also collected a ball signed by Cliff Lee and the bat Grady Sizemore used to hit a

# WALK-OFF WEEKEND - MAY 15-17

DURING THE FOUR-GAME SERIES AGAINST THE TWINS, THE YANKEES WALKED OFF WITH THREE STRAIGHT WINS IN THEIR FINAL AT-BAT, THE FIRST TIME THEY HAD ACCOMPLISHED SUCH A FEAT SINCE 1972. CABRERA CONTRIBUTED HIS SECOND WALK-OFF HIT TO START THE SERIES, THEN A-ROD BELTED A WALK-OFF HOMER THE NEXT DAY. DAMON JOINED THE FUN WITH A 10TH-INNING, GAME-WINNING HOMER IN THE THIRD GAME OF THE SERIES.

# RODRIGUEZ

"IT WAS A DREAM. IT'S BEEN TWO MONTHS, WHICH IS A LONG TIME. I'VE BEEN WATCHING A LOT OF BASEBALL, BEING VERY FRUSTRATED. I FEEL LIKE I'M BACK WITH MY FAMILY NOW, WHERE I BELONG."

—RODRIGUEZ

grand slam. But it wasn't until the next day that the Yankees won their first home game of the year. It would be the first of many.

The Yankees grew very comfortable in their new home, providing the first dramatic win less than a week later. Melky Cabrera hit a 14th-inning homer against the A's, treating fans to a walk-off win. Nine days later, Posada completed another one, hitting a two-run, bases-loaded single off Angels closer Brian Fuentes to cap a comeback from a five-run deficit.

"Hopefully we can grow from that," Posada said. "Hopefully we can learn that no lead is too big."

A week later, the Yankees had the first of two turning points in their season, and this one had to do with another type of comeback.

A-Rod returned to the lineup on May 8 in Baltimore, two months after the hip surgery that had cut his tumultuous spring short. Rodriguez didn't waste any time in

SWISHER

announcing his presence, crushing the first pitch he saw all season — a 98-mph Jeremy Guthrie fastball — into the left-field seats for a three-run homer.

"It was a dream," Rodriguez said. "It's

been two months, which is a long time. I've been watching a lot of baseball, being very frustrated. I feel like I'm back with my family now, where I belong."

For Nick Swisher, the scene was straight out of Hollywood.

"Amazing. Perfect. Storybook. Awesome," Swisher said afterward. "There was just a different aura today."

A-Rod's dramatic return grabbed the headlines, but just as important was the performance that night by Sabathia, who threw a complete-game shutout in the 4-0 win. It was the first by a Yankees pitcher in nearly three years. Following a 1-3 start in which his ERA was a pedestrian 4.85, Sabathia used the shutout to spark a 5-1 run over his next nine starts.

"Alex got us started off on the right foot, and CC took over," said manager Joe Girardi. "They were both exceptional performances."

# CABRERA

The Yankees went 90-44 starting May 8, posting the best record in the majors during that stretch, although they certainly experienced some bumps along the way.

The four-game series against the Twins the following week marked the most exciting weekend of the first half. The Yankees walked off with three straight wins, the first time they had accomplished such a feat since 1972. Cabrera contributed his second walk-off hit to start the series, then A-Rod belted a walk-off homer the next day. Damon joined the fun with a 10th-inning, game-winning homer in the third game of the series. It was the fifth walk-off victory for the Yankees in their first 16 games at the new Stadium, and all resulted in celebratory whipped cream pies to the face, courtesy of Burnett.

"We played some great baseball and so did [the Twins]," Girardi said. "We didn't win these games by a lot. They were very hot

coming in, so it was a nice job by our club."

The four-game sweep of the Twins was part of a nine-game winning streak that helped the Yankees slice five games off the Blue Jays' lead in the AL East. It marked the first of the Yankees' six winning streaks of

seven games or more, the most of any big-league team since the 1998 Yankees.

On May 29, the Yankees gained sole possession of first place in the division for the first time in 971 days, although Girardi was quick to take note of the work ahead.

"It doesn't mean a whole lot, but it's better than not being in first place," said the manager. "We know the goal is to be in first place on the last day of the season."

The Yankees and Red Sox traded the top two spots several times over the next seven weeks as Boston continued its early-season domination of the Bombers, completing a second three-game sweep at Fenway Park from June 9 through June 11 to claim victory in all eight first-half meetings between the two rivals.

The eight-game streak to start the season was the second-longest of all time for the Red Sox, bested only by their 14-game streak over the Yankees to start the 1912 season.

"It hasn't been fun for us against the Red Sox," Girardi said after the Yanks' third sweep at the hands of the BoSox. "The big picture is that we've got a long way to go. We have to leave it behind us. That's all you can do. In this game, you get used to turning the page. This is a resilient group; we've dealt with a lot and gotten back up every time. I don't expect this to be any different."

The Yankees appeared to turn things around when they returned home, taking two of three games against the Mets in memorable fashion. On June 12, A-Rod popped up what looked to be the final out of the game, but Mets second baseman Luis Castillo dropped the ball, allowing two runs to score for the most improbable win of the season.

"We feel like we stole one," Jeter said. "You never assume, but that's about as close as you can get to the game being over. You can see that play 1,000 more times and it probably won't happen again. We were lucky. That's the bottom line."

Two days later, the Yankees didn't need any late-inning bloopers, battering Johan Santana for a career-worst nine runs in a 15-0 romp to claim the Subway Series win.

"That's just the Subway Series," Girardi said. "You're going to see some strange

ROBINSON CANO

PHIL COKE

JERRY HAIRSTON

ALFREDO ACEVES

ERIC HINSKE

things. If someone would have told us that was how we would win two out of three, I'd have never guessed that."

They also never would have guessed they would suffer four losses in six games to the Marlins and Nationals, but that's what happened after the Mets series. A series-opening loss to the Braves in Atlanta on June 23 led to an impromptu visit from general manager Brian Cashman, who chal-

lenged his team to get back on the winning track and play to its potential.

"You could tell he meant business; he wasn't supposed to be here, but he flew down to Atlanta because we hadn't been playing well," Teixeira said. "Sometimes the principal needs to show up in the classroom if the teacher is having trouble with the students."

Hours after Cashman spoke with his

team, the Yankees were on their way to another lackluster performance. They played the first five innings against the Braves without putting a single runner on base. After finally getting a base runner in the sixth, Brett Gardner was picked off, prompting Girardi to argue the call. The fired-up manager was ejected, and his explosion seemed to wake up the Yankees.

Francisco Cervelli homered immediately

JOBA CHAMBERLAIN

JOSE MOLINA

CHAD GAUDIN

DAVID ROBERTSON

PHIL HUGHES

# RIVERA'S 500TH SAVE

**I**N THE JUNE 28 WIN OVER THE METS AT CITI FIELD, RIVERA RECORDED HIS 500TH CAREER SAVE, BECOMING ONLY THE SECOND RELIEVER TO REACH THE MILESTONE.

after Girardi's ejection, sparking an 8-4 victory in a game that served as the ultimate turning point for the Yankees.

"It could have been the spark plug," Teixeira said. "I love seeing a manager stick up for his team. It was a bad call, and Joe stood up for us. He knows we're battling out there, so he's going to go battle for us."

The June 24 win kicked off a stretch in which the Yankees won 13 of 15 games, highlighted by Rivera's 500th career save in the June 28 win over the Mets at Citi Field.

The Yankees finished the first half with a three-game sweep at the hands of the Angels, but the four-day All-Star break seemed to provide enough time to get the sweep out of their heads. The

Bombers won their first eight games and 11 of 13 to start the second half.

Having taken over first place for good on July 21, the Yankees were playing as well as they had all season, but a three-game skid against the White Sox in Chicago was cause for concern — especially with Mark Buehrle set to take the mound in the series finale just 10 days after he had thrown a perfect game.

Things looked bleak after Sabathia gave up four runs in the third to blow an early 3-0 lead, but Sabathia recovered to guide the Yankees to an 8-5 win. The win started another dominant run that saw the lefthander go 9-0 with a 2.04 ERA over 11 starts, giving him 19 total victories.

GIRARDI

"WE FEEL LIKE WE STOLE ONE. YOU NEVER ASSUME, BUT THAT'S ABOUT AS CLOSE AS YOU CAN GET TO THE GAME BEING OVER. YOU CAN SEE THAT PLAY 1,000 MORE TIMES AND IT PROBABLY WON'T HAPPEN AGAIN."
— JETER

RODRIGUEZ

BURNETT

TEIXEIRA

Sabathia got a major assist from Cabrera in the win over the White Sox. The outfielder became the first Yankees player since 1995 to hit for the cycle, finishing his historic night with a ninth-inning triple.

"It's a day [Cabrera will] never forget," A-Rod said. "We won't either."

The Yankees rode their momentum to a two-game sweep in Toronto, sending them home for a four-game series against the Red Sox on a high note. The offense exploded for 13 runs on 18 hits in the opener, pounding John Smoltz to finally end the Yanks' season-long misery against Boston.

"It's definitely better to be 1-8 than 0-9," said Damon, one of four Yankees to hit home runs in the win. "Obviously, we're happy about it, but those are eight games that we can't get back."

They did the next best thing, however, sweeping the four-game series to move 6 ½ games ahead of the Red Sox in the division. A-Rod provided the most memorable moment of the weekend in the second game of the series, smacking a two-run homer in the 15th inning of a scoreless game for the 10th walk-off victory of the season for the Yankees.

"It was like a playoff game," Girardi said. "There are going to be games like that down the stretch for us."

GARDNER

# JETER'S
## RECORD-BREAKING
# HIT

**O**N SEPT. 11, JETER LINED AN OPPOSITE-FIELD SINGLE AGAINST BALTIMORE'S CHRIS TILLMAN, MOVING PAST LOU GEHRIG FOR SOLE POSSESSION OF FIRST PLACE ON THE YANKEES' ALL-TIME HITS LIST.

The Yankees' lead over the Red Sox never dipped below five games for the rest of the season as the Bombers cruised toward their first AL East title since 2006.

But before they locked up their trip to the postseason, the Yankees witnessed one of the franchise's all-time greats chase down a legend.

On Sept. 11, Jeter lined an opposite-field single against Baltimore's Chris Tillman, moving past Lou Gehrig for sole possession of first place on the Yankees' all-time hits list.

"It's still hard to believe," Jeter said. "Being a Yankees fan, this is something I never imagined. Your dream is always to play for the team, and once you get here, you just want to stay and try to be consistent. This wasn't a part of it. This whole experience has been overwhelming."

The entire Yankees dugout emptied onto the field to congratulate Jeter as he acknowledged the raucous crowd with a few tips of his helmet.

"They caught me off guard," Jeter said of his teammates. "I didn't know what to do. For them to come out there, it was a special moment for me. It's a special moment for the organization, so to get to share it with my teammates was a lot of fun."

The Yankees punched their ticket to October with a Sept. 22 win in Anaheim, but it wasn't until they swept the Red Sox in their final meeting of the season that they popped the champagne. Their 100th win of the season on Sept. 27 locked up the AL East title and home-field advantage throughout the postseason on the same day.

"Winning a championship is what I came here for," Sabathia said. "It definitely feels good — first one in pinstripes, first one in the new Stadium, first celebration."

# TURNING POINT

Every championship season has its share of seminal moments, but for the 2009 Yankees, the night of June 24 may have served as a launching pad for their run to the World Series.

The Yankees came to Atlanta after dropping four out of six to the Nationals and Marlins, and after watching his team get shut out in its first game against the Braves, general manager Brian Cashman made an impromptu trip down south to rally the troops.

"You could tell he meant business; he wasn't supposed to be here, but he flew down to Atlanta because we hadn't been playing well," Mark Teixeira said. "Sometimes the principal needs to show up in the classroom if the teacher is having trouble with the students."

Five innings into that night's game, the Yankees hadn't put a runner on base, allowing a pair of Atlanta rookies to combine for five perfect frames. Brett Gardner finally broke it up with a leadoff walk in the sixth, but first base umpire Bill Welke called him out on a pickoff play, though replays showed Gardner was safe.

Joe Girardi argued the call in animated fashion, prompting Welke to eject him. Moments later, Francisco Cervelli belted his first career home run, sparking the Yankees to an 8-4 win. It was the first of seven consecutive wins for the Yankees, who went on to post a 13-2 record in their next 15 games and 21-5 record in their next 26 to help them pull away from the Red Sox in the AL East.

— MARK FEINSAND

# MARK
# TEIXEIRA

BY MARK FEINSAND

The expectations that come along with a mammoth free-agent contract are often impossible to meet. Not for Mark Teixeira — who delivered everything the Yankees could have hoped for in his first year in pinstripes, including a World Series title.

Teixeira wowed his new team with his steady bat and golden glove all season, filling the No. 3 spot in the lineup in impressive fashion. Teixeira led the American League in home runs, RBI and total bases, teaming with cleanup hitter Alex Rodriguez to form a lethal combination in the heart of the Yankees' batting order.

As one of three high-profile free agents brought in during the offseason, Teixeira knew that anything short of a World Series title would be considered a failure. It didn't take long for Teixeira, CC Sabathia and A.J. Burnett to become ingrained in the clubhouse, something that helped the trio feel comfortable in their pinstripes.

"From Day I, the veterans, the guys that have won championships here, have welcomed all of us with open arms,"

Teixeira said. "Sometimes that's hard. When you have a tight group, the outsiders come in and maybe they don't mesh. But that was not the case here."

Teixeira struggled out of the gate, hitting only .198 through the team's first 28 games of the season. But once A-Rod returned from hip surgery to back him up, Teixeira took off, batting .310 with 34 home runs and 107 RBI from that point forward.

Teixeira's numbers tapered off in the postseason, but the few hits he got were quite timely. His two hits in the American League Division Series came in Game 2, a single that set up A-Rod's game-tying homer in the ninth and a walk-off homer in the 11th that gave the Yankees a 4-3 win over the Twins.

Then, after another slow start in the

American League Championship Series, Teixeira hit a three-run double in Game 5 and contributed a big sacrifice fly in the Yankees' Game 6 clincher against the Angels. Teixeira had only three hits in the Yankees' six World Series games, but two of them drove in runs, including a Game 2 home run against Pedro Martinez and an RBI single in the Game 6 clincher.

"Every season I get home and I look at the stats, and I say, 'Man, that's nice.' But I'm watching the World Series," Teixeira said. "I don't care about what I did in the playoffs because it's about the team winning a championship. For the rest of my life, I can say I played on a world championship New York Yankees team."

# A.J. BURNETT

BY MARK FEINSAND

## A.J. Burnett's first year in pinstripes was as easy as pie.

The righthander established a new tradition by delivering a whipped cream pie in the face of any teammate who contributed a walk-off hit, adding some playfulness to a clubhouse that had long been described as being too corporate.

But as much of an impact as Burnett had on the Yankees' personality, the talented 32-year-old also got the job done on the mound. He followed up his 13-win season with the first postseason run of his 11-year career, doing his part to lead the Bombers to the World Series crown.

Burnett was anxious before taking the mound in Game 2 of the American League Division Series against the Twins, but after harnessing his emotions during the final month of the regular season, he was ready to take the ball under the brightest of lights.

"I've always said I'm ready for the stage," Burnett said the day before Game 2. "I plan on backing that up. It's going to be crazy."

Burnett did just that, giving up one run over six innings in his postseason debut. The game was tied, 1-1, when he left, but after the Twins took a two-run lead in the eighth, Burnett watched Alex Rodriguez hit a game-tying, two-run homer in the ninth, setting up Mark Teixeira's 11th-inning walk-off homer — and another of Burnett's special pies.

Burnett took another no-decision in his next postseason start, a 6 1/3-inning, two-run effort in Game 2 of the American League Championship Series against the Angels. The Yankees went on to win in 13 innings, but Burnett failed to clinch the series in Game 5, experiencing his first hiccup of the postseason as the Angels scored six runs against him in six innings.

The Yankees closed out the Angels in six games, giving Burnett the chance to pitch in his first World Series, something he longed for ever since 2003, when he watched his Marlins teammates win the title as he rehabbed from elbow surgery.

In his fourth start of the postseason, Burnett finally earned that coveted first victory, beating the Phillies in Game 2 with seven brilliant innings. Burnett struck out nine while allowing one run, pulling the Yankees even in the Series after Philadelphia had taken Game 1. For the second consecutive series, he couldn't close it out in Game 5, but when Andy Pettitte led the Yankees to a Game 6 win to wrap up the title, Burnett made good on a season-long promise, delivering one final pie — to manager Joe Girardi.

"I told him I was going to get him if we won it all — and I did," Burnett said, wiping champagne from his eyes. "I don't think he minded."

# THE CORE

BY BOB KLAPISCH

Derek Jeter slung his arm around Mariano Rivera for all the world to see, finally lowering the walls of his soul. The captain — the Prime Minister of Cool — no longer cared about appearances, not with a world championship party raging in the clubhouse and the entire Yankees family now in a barely controlled state of delirium.

Everyone, it seemed, had a reason to go crazy after Game 6 of the World Series. Joe Girardi had just notched his first title as manager, Alex Rodriguez picked up his first ring ever, and the newcomers — CC Sabathia, A.J. Burnett and Mark Teixeira — had bodysurfed along with the most successful franchise in sports history.

"Awesome" is what Sabathia kept repeating into the cameras.

"People told me, 'Man, there's nothing like winning in New York,'" said the southpaw. "Now I know what they were talking about."

All the big lefthander had to do was ask Jeter or Rivera or Andy Pettitte or Jorge Posada. They've been around for a million or so years and have the winning pedigree

to prove it. For all the Yankees who partied into the early morning hours after their victory on Nov. 4, 2009, none had a greater appreciation for championship No. 27 — the first since 2000 — than the four core players who started winning in 1996.

"I grew up with these guys in the minor leagues," Jeter said, almost in disbelief. "It's one thing to play 17 years. It's another to

"I GREW UP WITH THESE GUYS IN THE MINOR LEAGUES. IT'S ONE THING TO PLAY 17 YEARS. IT'S ANOTHER TO PLAY THAT LONG WITH THE SAME GUYS."

— JETER

play that long with the same guys."

The captain was right. In this era of free agency and ever-changing rosters, it's a near impossibility that the same four players could win five championships together. In fact, no player had won five titles with the Yankees since Yogi Berra (10 titles), Mickey Mantle (seven) and Whitey Ford (six) won their last title in 1962.

Historians have to go back almost 50 years to find a comparison to this Yankees core. The Bombers won 10 championships between 1947 and '62, and according to the Elias Sports Bureau, 21 players shared in at

*Pettitte*

least four of those titles. The fact that so many Yankees had been nurtured in the same farm system made a difference, said Berra.

The same can be said of the franchise's current guardians. Pettitte and Posada were both drafted in 1990, the year Rivera was signed as a free agent. Jeter joined the organization two years later as a first-round draft pick.

They followed the same trail, from Greensboro, North Carolina, to Prince William County, Virginia, finally coming together in 1994 at Triple-A Columbus in Ohio. By the time the Core Four arrived

*Pettitte*

# "WE WERE BROTHERS."

— RIVERA

Jeter

in New York, they already shared a bond.

"We were brothers," said Rivera.

Each of them remembers the good old days, although youth wasn't always kind to the core. Jeter was just a skinny, unobtrusive rookie in 1996, so awkward and overly polite that he referred to his manager as "Mr. Torre." Pettitte, drafted out of San Jacinto College in Texas, was only 26 starts into his career. Rivera was still only a set-up man to then-closer John Wetteland, and Posada, who had started his career as a second baseman, was called up late in the first championship season and wasn't even added to the postseason roster.

Today they're older, wiser, a little fleshier in the face perhaps, but otherwise defying the laws of nature. Even at age 39, Rivera continues to throw the single most devastating pitch in the game's history, his cut fastball. It has propelled him to a career 0.74 ERA in the postseason, a feat that may never be matched. But Rivera believes he still has unfinished business in October.

"I think I can play for five more years," he told the Yankee Stadium crowd after Game 6.

The fans, woozy from the scent of victory, never thought twice about that declaration. They merely roared in approval.

It was, after all, the perfect night to crash through barriers — the Phillies, the laws of nature, logic. Pettitte had started and

*Posada*

# "I THINK I CAN PLAY FOR FIVE MORE YEARS."
## — RIVERA

*Posada [L] and Rivera*

*Jeter [L] and Posada*

won the decisive game against Philadelphia, Rivera finished it off, and Posada and Jeter were both on the field for the final out. The symmetry was almost surreal.

Along the way, Posada had morphed from Girardi's backup catcher to a perennial All-Star whose career path may wind its way into Cooperstown. Pettitte, working in the shadow of David Cone, Roger Clemens and most recently Sabathia, had turned into a latter-day Chairman of the Board, collecting a major league-record 18 postseason victories. Rivera had long since become the greatest closer of all time — with disputes — while Jeter had turned into a once-in-a-generation icon in New York.

Jeter is often compared to Joe DiMaggio

for his grace and inexhaustible reservoir of cool, but there was another legend on Jeter's mind in the summer of '09. He caught and passed Lou Gehrig as the franchise's all-time leader in hits, a mark Jeter cherished for symbolic value.

"To think about the way Lou Gehrig lived his life and the way he carried himself on the field, it meant a lot to me," Jeter said after recording his record-breaking 2,722nd hit on Sept. 11.

It was hard to believe this was the same player who had made nine errors in his first 11 games as a rookie at Single-A 17 years ago. Pettitte, who was on that team, recalled thinking, "This is our first-round draft pick?"

Jeter just smiles now at the memory,

even if no one will let him forget about it. The new millennium has taught the captain a thing or two about humor, but mostly, it has rearranged his priorities as a leader in Girardi's clubhouse.

"Derek will remind a player in batting practice to work on hitting to the opposite field instead of trying to hit home runs," said the manager, who added that Rivera handled a similar responsibility with the relief corps.

"If someone is talking about having to pitch two consecutive days or doesn't like the way he's being used, [Rivera] will tell him to worry about pitching only when they are called upon," Girardi said.

Those are the subtle gifts of experience, and you don't have to ask Girardi

*Rivera*

# "IT'S HARD TO BELIEVE THAT AFTER ALL THESE YEARS, WE'RE STILL HERE. THERE'S NO DOUBT WINNING IS SWEETER THIS WAY."

### — PETTITTE

how much he appreciates them. His core players made it possible for the newcomers — Sabathia, Burnett and Teixeira — to assimilate in New York's overheated environment. Pettitte, for one, ended up with the nickname "The Godfather" because of his wisdom. That been-there, done-that vibe is friendly, reassuring, almost intoxicating to anyone stepping into the cauldron for the first time.

"Definitely, Andy has made it easier for me," Teixeira said. "He's always there, always easy to talk to. One of the great things about being a Yankee is that there are guys here who've been around for a long time and can tell you what to expect."

Pettitte earned that education the hard way — after 12 years on the game's biggest stage. But he was never alone. He had Jeter, Posada and Rivera with him all along, which made for a historic ride and an especially poignant celebration in 2009.

"It's hard to believe that after all these years, we're still here," Pettitte said. "There's no doubt winning is sweeter this way."

*Pettitte*

# CC SABATHIA

BY MARK FEINSAND

CC Sabathia couldn't secure a victory in the first regular-season game ever played at the new Yankee Stadium. When he took the mound for the Stadium's first postseason contest, he came through.

From the moment Sabathia fired his first pitch against the Twins in Game 1 of the American League Division Series, the hulking lefthander stepped up his game and put the Yankees on his broad back, carrying them to victory with one dominant postseason performance after another.

"This is what you come here for, to pitch in the postseason and play in October," Sabathia said after giving up one earned run over 6 2/3 innings in his first postseason game in pinstripes. "It was electric tonight."

The same could be said for Sabathia, who lived up to expectations in his debut season in the Bronx. The big southpaw won 19 games to tie for the major league lead, then set the tone for the Yankees' first-round sweep of the Twins.

When he took the ball to open the American League Championship Series

against the Angels, Sabathia had a tougher task ahead of him. The Angels had roughed him up twice during the regular season, but Sabathia came out like a man on a mission in Game 1, cruising through eight innings of one-run ball to get the Yankees started on the right foot for a second consecutive series.

Sabathia came back on short rest to take the ball in Game 4, repeating his stellar performance with another eight-inning, one-run outing to give the Yankees a commanding 3-games-to-1 lead.

The Yankees went on to win the pennant in six games with Sabathia earning ALCS MVP honors for his 2-0 record and 1.12 ERA. It also erased any questions that may have existed about Sabathia's ability to thrive in the postseason, where his record prior to 2009 had been shaky at best.

"I never had any doubt about me being able to perform on this stage, to pitch well in October, but it seemed like people did," Sabathia said. "I feel great, and hopefully, I can keep it going."

Sabathia was outdueled by former teammate Cliff Lee in Game 1 of the World Series, but he came back on short rest — again — to give the Yankees a solid effort in Game 4, grinding his way through 6 2/3 innings before the Bombers won the game in the ninth.

Three days later, Sabathia watched as Andy Pettitte closed out the Phillies in Game 6, finishing off a memorable debut season for the Yankees' new ace.

"It's unbelievable," Sabathia said. "This is what you play for."

# POSTSEASON

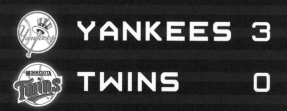

YANKEES 3

TWINS 0

# GROUP EFFORT

BY KRISTINA M. DODGE

## SOLID PITCHING AND TIMELY HITTING
## EQUAL VICTORY IN POSTSEASON OPENER

TWINS **2** YANKEES **7**

**D**erek Jeter continued his assault on the record books, CC Sabathia and Alex Rodriguez proved postseason pressure was not a factor, and Mariano Rivera closed out the ballgame as the Yankees overtook the Twins, 7-2, in Game 1 of the American League Division Series at Yankee Stadium.

"It was big for us, especially when you're playing a five-game series," said Jeter, who went 2-for-2 with two walks. "Every game is important. You want to come out here, you want to play well, [and] you want to sort of set the tone."

Which Jeter did almost single-handedly with a two-run, third-inning home run that evened the score, lit a fire under his teammates and gave Yankee Stadium its first building-shaking postseason moment. Game 1 marked the first October game in the new Yankee Stadium and the Yankees' 14th postseason appearance in 15 seasons.

"It felt just like the old place," said Jeter.

The Twins had clinched the Central Division crown in a 12-inning tiebreaker less than 24 hours earlier, but generated enough energy to take an early lead and break up a scoreless ballgame. In the third inning, they tagged Sabathia for two runs, their only runs of the night, before Jeter gave the Yankees the jumpstart they needed.

In the bottom of the inning, the captain blasted one into the left-field seats off of Minnesota starter Brian Duensing for his 18th career postseason home run, tying Reggie Jackson and Mickey Mantle for third place on baseball's all-time postseason list.

"The place got loud," said Sabathia. "Him starting out the game with a single and then tying the score up right back, it just made me want to go out there and get three quick outs and try to get these guys back in the dugout and score some more runs."

Over the next four innings, the Yanks proceeded to tack on five runs. Nick Swisher put the Bombers in the lead with an RBI double in the fourth inning. In the fifth, Hideki Matsui added to the 13 home runs he hit against lefthanded pitchers during the regular season by lacing a two-run shot off reliever Francisco Liriano, and Rodriguez snapped an 0-for-19 postseason funk with runners in scoring posi-

tion when he hit RBI singles in the fifth and seventh innings.

"Everyone wants to contribute, and I thought the key for us tonight was we got five RBIs with two outs," said manager Joe Girardi. "We got two from Alex, two from Matsui and one from Swish. Those are big hits."

Sabathia entered his first postseason in pinstripes with six career October starts to his name and temporarily quieted critics who pointed out his high walk count in postseasons past: 22 batters in 25 innings. The lefty issued no walks while allowing one earned run on eight hits and striking out eight in 6 2/3 innings. His first three frames were shaky, as he gave up a

*Rodriguez*

SABATHIA SETTLED
IN AND RETIRED
12 OF THE LAST 15
BATTERS HE FACED.
HE LEFT TO
A STANDING
OVATION.

# MATSUI

## A HIT FROM THE DH SPOT WHEN CC'S ON THE MOUND

**H**ideki Matsui's two-run blast in the fifth inning of Game 1 didn't just help the Yankees pull away from the Twins. It continued a trend that CC Sabathia hoped would never end.

The lefthanded swinging slugger hit safely in the last nine regular-season games in which he was the starting designated hitter and Sabathia was on the mound, batting .421 (16-for-38) with six home runs and 15 RBI.

"That guy is unbelievable," Sabathia said after the game. "I probably had 30 starts; he's probably hit a home run in 25 of them. Lefties, righties, no matter who you put out there, he takes good swings off of them."

The Yanks' 7-2 victory was their 10th straight win with both Sabathia and Matsui in the starting lineup.

— Nathan Maciborski

leadoff double in the first and worked deep into counts, and miscommunication with battery mate Jorge Posada resulted in two passed balls, one of which cost the team a run. But after a two-out RBI single to Michael Cuddyer in the third, Sabathia settled in and retired 12 of the last 15 batters he faced. He left to a standing ovation.

"CC has been pretty consistent the entire year," said Jeter. "He's a guy, even when he gets in trouble, he's capable of getting a big

strikeout, getting out of jams. We have a lot of confidence when he's on the mound. He pitched another great game for us today [and did] exactly what we needed him to do."

Phil Hughes, Phil Coke and Joba Chamberlain combined for a scoreless 1⅓ innings before "Enter Sandman" ushered in Rivera. Mo hadn't pitched since the team's last regular-season game on Oct. 4 and wouldn't have another opportunity until Game 2 on Oct. 9. The closer allowed one walk and one hit with two outs

before getting Orlando Cabrera to ground out to second to end the inning in the non-save situation.

"We did a lot of good things today," said Jeter. "Our pitching staff starting with CC, our bullpen was good. Mo closed it out. We swung the bats well. We hit a couple of home runs. We couldn't have drawn it up any better."

| MINNESOTA | AB | R | H | RBI | BB | SO | LOB | AVG |
|---|---|---|---|---|---|---|---|---|
| Span, CF | 5 | 0 | 2 | 0 | 0 | 1 | 3 | .400 |
| Cabrera, SS | 5 | 1 | 2 | 0 | 0 | 2 | 5 | .400 |
| Mauer, C | 4 | 1 | 2 | 0 | 0 | 1 | 2 | .500 |
| Cuddyer, 1B | 4 | 0 | 1 | 1 | 0 | 1 | 2 | .250 |
| Kubel, RF | 4 | 0 | 0 | 0 | 0 | 2 | 2 | .000 |
| Young, LF | 4 | 0 | 0 | 0 | 0 | 2 | 1 | .000 |
| Harris, DH | 4 | 0 | 1 | 0 | 0 | 2 | 0 | .250 |
| Tolbert, 3B | 3 | 0 | 0 | 0 | 0 | 1 | 1 | .000 |
| Punto, 2B | 3 | 0 | 2 | 0 | 1 | 0 | 0 | .667 |
| TOTALS | 36 | 2 | 10 | 1 | 1 | 12 | 16 | |

**BATTING:**
2B: Span (1, Sabathia); Mauer (1, Sabathia). TB: Span 3; Cabrera 2; Mauer 3; Cuddyer; Harris; Punto 2. RBI: Cuddyer (1). 2-out RBI: Cuddyer. Runners left in scoring position, 2 out: Cabrera 4; Mauer; Cuddyer; Kubel. GIDP: Span Team LOB: 9.

**BASERUNNING:**
SB: Cabrera (1, 2nd base off Sabathia/Posada).

**FIELDING:**
E: Cuddyer (1, ground ball). DP: 1 (Tolbert-Punto-Cuddyer).

| N.Y. YANKEES | AB | R | H | RBI | BB | SO | LOB | AVG |
|---|---|---|---|---|---|---|---|---|
| Jeter, SS | 2 | 3 | 2 | 2 | 2 | 0 | 0 | 1.000 |
| Damon, LF | 4 | 0 | 1 | 0 | 0 | 0 | 2 | .250 |
| Teixeira, 1B | 4 | 0 | 0 | 0 | 0 | 0 | 5 | .000 |
| Rodriguez, 3B | 4 | 1 | 2 | 2 | 0 | 1 | 2 | .500 |
| Matsui, DH | 3 | 1 | 1 | 2 | 1 | 0 | 0 | .333 |
| Posada, C | 4 | 0 | 1 | 0 | 0 | 1 | 2 | .250 |
| Cano, 2B | 4 | 1 | 0 | 0 | 0 | 1 | 1 | .000 |
| Swisher, RF | 4 | 0 | 1 | 1 | 0 | 0 | 0 | .250 |
| Gardner, CF | 0 | 0 | 0 | 0 | 0 | 0 | 0 | .000 |
| Cabrera, CF-RF | 4 | 1 | 1 | 0 | 0 | 2 | 1 | .250 |
| TOTALS | 33 | 7 | 9 | 7 | 3 | 5 | 13 | |

**BATTING:**
2B: Swisher (1, Duensing). HR: Jeter (1, 3rd inning off Duensing, 1 on, 1 out); Matsui (1, 5th inning off Liriano, 1 on, 2 out). TB: Jeter 5; Damon; Rodriguez 2; Matsui 4; Posada; Swisher 2; Cabrera. RBI: Jeter 2; Rodriguez 2; Matsui 2; Swisher. 2-out RBI: Rodriguez 2; Matsui 2; Swisher. Runners left in scoring position, 2 out: Rodriguez; Posada; Cabrera. GIDP: Teixeira. Team LOB: 5.

| | | |
|---|---|---|
| MINNESOTA TWINS | | 2 |
| NEW YORK YANKEES | | 7 |

| | 1 | 2 | 3 | 4 | 5 | 6 | 7 | 8 | 9 | | R | H | E |
|---|---|---|---|---|---|---|---|---|---|---|---|---|---|
| TWINS | 0 | 0 | 2 | 0 | 0 | 0 | 0 | 0 | 0 | | 2 | 10 | 1 |
| YANKEES | 0 | 0 | 2 | 1 | 3 | 0 | 1 | 0 | X | | 7 | 9 | 0 |

FIELDING:
PB: Posada 2.
DP: 1 (Rodriguez-Cano-Teixeira).

| MINNESOTA | IP | H | R | ER | BB | SO | HR | ERA |
|---|---|---|---|---|---|---|---|---|
| Duensing (L, 0-1) | 4⅔ | 7 | 5 | 5 | 1 | 3 | 1 | 9.64 |
| Liriano | 2 | 1 | 2 | 1 | 1 | 1 | 1 | 4.50 |
| Rauch | ⅓ | 1 | 0 | 0 | 1 | 0 | 0 | 0.00 |
| Mahay | 1 | 0 | 0 | 0 | 0 | 1 | 0 | 0.00 |

| N.Y. YANKEES | IP | H | R | ER | BB | SO | HR | ERA |
|---|---|---|---|---|---|---|---|---|
| Sabathia (W, 1-0) | 6⅔ | 8 | 2 | 1 | 0 | 8 | 0 | 1.35 |
| Hughes (H, 1) | ⅔ | 1 | 0 | 0 | 0 | 2 | 0 | 0.00 |
| Coke | ⅓ | 0 | 0 | 0 | 0 | 0 | 0 | 0.00 |
| Chamberlain | ⅓ | 0 | 0 | 0 | 0 | 0 | 0 | 0.00 |
| Rivera | 1 | 1 | 0 | 0 | 1 | 2 | 0 | 0.00 |

WP: Duensing. Sabathia.
HBP: Tolbert (by Sabathia).

Pitches-strikes: Duensing 79-59; Liriano 35-19; Rauch 9-3; Mahay 14-9. Sabathia 113-71; Hughes 24-16; Coke 1-1; Chamberlain 2-1; Rivera 23-13.

Ground outs-fly outs: Duensing 6-5; Liriano 3-2; Rauch 1-0; Mahay 1-1. Sabathia 5-7; Hughes 0-0; Coke 0-1; Chamberlain 1-0; Rivera 1-0.

Batters faced: Duensing 22; Liriano 8; Rauch 3; Mahay 3. Sabathia 28; Hughes 3; Coke 1; Chamberlain 1; Rivera 5.
Inherited runners-scored: Liriano 1-1; Rauch 1-1. Hughes 2-0; Coke 1-0; Chamberlain 1-0.

Umpires: HP: Tim Tschida. 1B: Chuck Meriwether. 2B: Mark Wegner. 3B: Paul Emmel. LF: Jim Joyce. RF: Phil Cuzzi.

Weather: 62 degrees, cloudy. Wind: 24 mph. T: 3:38. Att: 49,464.

# DRAMA KINGS

BY NATHAN MACIBORSKI

## A-ROD, TEIXEIRA DRIVING FORCE BEHIND YANKEES' ALDS GAME 2 VICTORY

TWINS  YANKEES

**A**fter scaring the monkey off his back in Game 1 of the American League Division Series, Alex Rodriguez ran that monkey clear out of town in Game 2.

Rodriguez blasted a game-tying, two-run home run in the ninth inning, then celebrated from the on-deck circle in the 11th as Mark Teixeira ripped a walk-off job over the fence in left field for a 4-3 Yankees win.

"I think the first hit [in Game 1] was one that definitely made me feel like I checked in and started contributing a little bit," said Rodriguez, who had batted just .143 (8-for-56) with one RBI over his previous 16 postseason games. "I feel great — not only with the game, but in my life."

Teixeira's first career postseason homer, which came in his first career at-bat against Jose Mijares, gave the Yankees their 16th walk-off victory of the season and the team's fourth against Minnesota. David Robertson earned the victory after wiggling out of a bases-loaded, no-out jam in the top of the 11th.

TEIXEIRA'S FIRST CAREER POSTSEASON HOMER GAVE THE YANKEES THEIR 16TH WALK-OFF VICTORY OF THE SEASON AND THE TEAM'S FOURTH AGAINST MINNESOTA.

"That was incredible," Teixeira said. "Bases loaded, game on the line, maybe series on the line with how well these guys play in Minnesota, coming up with three big outs in a row, that's impressive for a young pitcher."

The late-game heroics of the Yankees' fearsome 3-4 punch relegated solid outings by both starters to mere footnotes. Making the first postseason appearance of his 11-year career, Yankees righthander A.J. Burnett faced 27 batters over six innings, allowing just three hits and one run while striking out six and walking five.

Twins righty Nick Blackburn held the Yanks hitless until Robinson Cano's two-out single in the fifth and led 1-0 until the sixth, when A-Rod delivered a big two-out RBI single.

With both starters gone and the score tied, 1-1, Game 2 became a battle of the bullpens. Earlier in the day, the Twins' Joe Nathan and the Yankees' Mariano Rivera were named co-winners of the 2009 American League Rolaids Relief Man Award — the first tie in the award's 33-year history. Both firemen were called into action in Game 2 with Rivera getting

# ROBERTSON
## PUTS ON MAGICAL PERFORMANCE

**W**ho knew Harry Houdini donned the pinstripes? In his postseason debut, 24-year-old David Robertson escaped a bases-loaded, nobody-out jam in the top of the 11th inning to keep the game knotted at 3-3.

Robertson entered the game with runners on first and second and subsequently yielded a crisp single up the middle to Michael Cuddyer to load the bases. Then, Robertson's wizardry began. The righty got Delmon Young to line

out to first baseman Mark Teixeira, Carlos Gomez to ground out weakly to Teixeira, who threw home to force Joe Mauer, and Brendan Harris to fly out to Brett Gardner — stranding three baserunners and setting the stage for Teixeira's walk-off solo homer to lead off the bottom half of the frame.

"Nobody really wants to get stuck in that situation," Robertson said. "I was just lucky enough to get out of it."

— Craig Tapper

four outs after the Twins tagged Phil Hughes for two runs in the top of the eighth and Nathan coming in to close out a 3-1 ballgame in the ninth.

Nathan — who faced the Yankees once during the regular season on May 15, when he allowed three ninth-inning runs in a 5-4 loss — promptly gave up a line-drive single to Teixeira to start the ninth, then fell behind A-Rod, 3-0.

After taking an inside fastball for a called strike, Rodriguez unloaded on Nathan's fifth offering — a belt-high 94-mph fastball — and sent it deep into the Yankees bullpen in right-center. Rodriguez looked to his teammates celebrating in the dugout as he trotted down the first-base line and let out a roar as he headed home.

"Since I've been [back], there's been a lot of magic in there and everybody has contributed," Rodriguez said. "But for me personally, that was obviously a lot of fun."

*Teixeira*

ALDS 2009 — GAME 2

| MINNESOTA TWINS | 3 |
| NEW YORK YANKEES | 4 |

| | 1 | 2 | 3 | 4 | 5 | 6 | 7 | 8 | 9 | 10 | 11 | R | H | E |
|---|---|---|---|---|---|---|---|---|---|---|---|---|---|
| TWINS | 0 | 0 | 0 | 0 | 0 | 1 | 0 | 2 | 0 | 0 | 0 | 3 | 12 | 1 |
| YANKEES | 0 | 0 | 0 | 0 | 0 | 1 | 0 | 0 | 2 | 0 | 1 | 4 | 7 | 0 |

| MINNESOTA | AB | R | H | RBI | BB | SO | LOB | AVG |
|---|---|---|---|---|---|---|---|---|
| Span, RF | 6 | 0 | 2 | 1 | 0 | 0 | 1 | .364 |
| Cabrera, SS | 5 | 0 | 0 | 0 | 1 | 1 | 5 | .200 |
| Mauer, C | 4 | 0 | 2 | 0 | 2 | 2 | 1 | .500 |
| Kubel, DH | 6 | 0 | 1 | 0 | 0 | 4 | 4 | .100 |
| Cuddyer, 1B | 6 | 0 | 3 | 0 | 0 | 0 | 0 | .400 |
| Young, LF | 4 | 1 | 0 | 0 | 1 | 2 | 5 | .000 |
| Gomez, CF | 4 | 1 | 0 | 0 | 1 | 2 | 5 | .000 |
| Tolbert, 3B | 2 | 0 | 1 | 0 | 0 | 0 | 1 | .200 |
| Harris, PH-3B | 4 | 1 | 2 | 1 | 0 | 0 | 3 | .375 |
| Punto, 2B | 3 | 0 | 1 | 1 | 2 | 1 | 1 | .500 |
| TOTALS | 44 | 3 | 12 | 3 | 7 | 12 | 26 | |

**BATTING:**
3B: Harris (1, Burnett). TB: Span 2; Mauer 2; Kubel; Cuddyer 3; Tolbert; Harris 4; Punto. RBI: Span (1); Harris (1); Punto (1). 2-out RBI: Span, Harris, Punto. Runners left in scoring position, 2 out: Cabrera 2; Kubel; Tolbert; Harris 2; Punto. Team LOB: 17.

**BASERUNNING:**
SB: Young (1, 2nd base off Burnett/Molina).

**FIELDING:**
E: Nathan (1, pickoff). DP: 1 (Cabrera-Harris).

| N.Y. YANKEES | AB | R | H | RBI | BB | SO | LOB | AVG |
|---|---|---|---|---|---|---|---|---|
| Jeter, SS | 4 | 1 | 1 | 0 | 1 | 0 | 0 | .500 |
| Damon, LF | 4 | 0 | 0 | 0 | 1 | 0 | 2 | .125 |
| Cervelli, C | 0 | 0 | 0 | 0 | 0 | 0 | 0 | .000 |
| Teixeira, 1B | 5 | 2 | 2 | 1 | 0 | 0 | 2 | .222 |
| Rodriguez, 3B | 4 | 1 | 2 | 3 | 0 | 0 | 0 | .500 |
| Matsui, DH | 3 | 0 | 0 | 0 | 1 | 1 | 2 | .167 |
| Swisher, RF | 4 | 0 | 0 | 0 | 0 | 1 | 1 | .125 |
| Cano, 2B | 4 | 0 | 1 | 0 | 0 | 0 | 1 | .125 |
| Cabrera, CF-LF | 4 | 0 | 0 | 0 | 0 | 1 | 1 | .125 |
| Molina, C | 1 | 0 | 0 | 0 | 0 | 0 | 0 | .000 |
| Posada, PH-C | 3 | 0 | 1 | 0 | 0 | 1 | 0 | .286 |
| Gardner, PR-CF | 0 | 0 | 0 | 0 | 0 | 0 | 0 | .000 |
| TOTALS | 36 | 4 | 7 | 4 | 3 | 4 | 9 | |

# BURNETT
## MAKES FIRST POSTSEASON START

**S**eason-ending elbow surgery early in 2003 prevented A.J. Burnett from taking the mound when his team, the Florida Marlins, made its world championship run. Six years later, he finally got his October moment.

The Yankees righthander made his first postseason appearance in Game 2, limiting the Twins to one run on three hits over six innings. The righty earned a no-decision in the Yankees' 4-3 victory.

"One run over six innings, what else can you ask for?" said battery mate Jose Molina. "He pitched an awesome game."

Despite praise for his outing, two hit batsmen and five walks had Burnett feeling as if he could have done more, but the experience itself exceeded all expectations.

"They could have given up on me with the five walks and two hit batters, but they stayed with me; this place was going nuts," Burnett told the *New York Daily News*. "Hearing the fans and the crowd, they were pretty loud, and I hadn't even stepped on the field yet. This is the best place to play. These people here, this place is amazing."

— Kristina M. Dodge

---

**BATTING:**
2B: Jeter (1, Blackburn). HR: Rodriguez (1, 9th inning off Nathan 1 on, 0 out); Teixeira (1, 11th inning off Mijares 0 on, 0 out). TB: Jeter 2; Teixeira 5; Rodriguez 5; Cano; Posada. RBI: Teixeira (1); Rodriguez 3 (5). 2-out RBI: Rodriguez; Runners left in scoring position, 2 out: Matsui. LIDP: Damon. Team LOB: 5.

**BASERUNNING:**
SB: Gardner (1, 2nd base off Nathan/Mauer).

**FIELDING:**
Outfield assists: Swisher (Gomez at 3rd base).

| MINNESOTA | IP | H | R | ER | BB | SO | HR | ERA |
|---|---|---|---|---|---|---|---|---|
| Blackburn | 5⅓ | 3 | 1 | 1 | 2 | 3 | 0 | 1.59 |
| Mahay | ⅓ | 0 | 0 | 0 | 0 | 0 | 0 | 0.00 |
| Rauch | 1 | 0 | 0 | 0 | 0 | 0 | 0 | 0.00 |
| Guerrier (H, 1) | 1 | 0 | 0 | 0 | 0 | 1 | 0 | 0.00 |
| Nathan (BS, 1) | 1⅓ | 3 | 2 | 2 | 1 | 0 | 1 | 13.50 |
| Mijares (L, 0-1) | ⅔ | 1 | 1 | 1 | 0 | 0 | 1 | 13.50 |
| N.Y. YANKEES | IP | H | R | ER | BB | SO | HR | ERA |
| Burnett | 6 | 3 | 1 | 1 | 5 | 6 | 0 | 1.50 |
| Chamberlain | ⅔ | 1 | 0 | 0 | 0 | 0 | 0 | 0.00 |
| Coke | ⅓ | 0 | 0 | 0 | 0 | 1 | 0 | 0.00 |
| Hughes | ⅔ | 2 | 2 | 2 | 1 | 1 | 0 | 13.50 |
| Rivera | 1⅓ | 2 | 0 | 0 | 0 | 3 | 0 | 0.00 |
| Aceves | 1 | 1 | 0 | 0 | 1 | 1 | 0 | 0.00 |
| Marte | 0 | 2 | 0 | 0 | 0 | 0 | 0 | 0.00 |
| Robertson (W, 1-0) | 1 | 1 | 0 | 0 | 0 | 0 | 0 | 0.00 |

Marte pitched to two batters in the 11th.
Mijares pitched to one batter in the 11th.

IBB: Jeter (by Nathan) HBP: Young (by Burnett); Gomez (by Burnett).
Pitches-strikes: Blackburn 92-56; Mahay 2-2; Rauch 14-8; Guerrier 12-8; Nathan 27-14; Mijares 10-5. Burnett 95-57; Chamberlain 11-6; Coke 5-3; Hughes 22-15; Rivera 27-19; Aceves 19-13; Marte 10-6; Robertson 9-7.

Ground outs-fly outs: Blackburn 7-7; Mahay 1-0; Rauch 1-2; Guerrier 2-0; Nathan 2-2; Mijares 0-1. Burnett 8-3; Chamberlain 2-0; Coke 0-0; Hughes 0-1; Rivera 0-1; Aceves 0-2; Marte 0-0; Robertson 1-2.

Batters Faced: Blackburn 22; Mahay 1; Rauch 3; Guerrier 3; Nathan 8; Mijares 2. Burnett 27; Chamberlain 3; Coke 1; Hughes 5; Rivera 6; Aceves 5; Marte 2; Robertson 4.
Inherited runners-scored: Mahay 2-0; Mijares 2-0. Coke 1-0; Rivera 2-1; Robertson 2-0.

Umpires: HP: Chuck Meriwether 1B: Mark Wegner. 2B: Paul Emmel. 3B: Jim Joyce. LF: Phil Cuzzi. RF: Tim Tschida.

Weather: 68 degrees, cloudy. T: 4:22 Att: 50,006.

# IT'S A
# SWEEP

BY ALFRED SANTASIERE III

## YANKS TAKE ALDS IN THREE BEHIND STRONG OUTING FROM PETTITTE

YANKEES **4** TWINS **1**

It took six innings, but the Yankees got Twins starter Carl Pavano's number, tagging him for two runs — longballs off the bats of Alex Rodriguez and Jorge Posada — on their way to sweeping the Twins with a 4-1 victory in Game 3 of the American League Division Series. The win put the Yankees in the American League Championship Series for the first time since 2004.

"This is what you play for," Derek Jeter said as his teammates doused each other with champagne in the moments after the game. "Now, we're playing for the opportunity to go to the World Series. It's only going to get more difficult as we go on, but we have a very talented team."

The game was scoreless for five innings as Yankees veteran Andy Pettitte matched Pavano in a classic pitcher's duel.

Pettitte retired all but one Twins hitter he faced during the first five innings while striking out five. He was economical, throwing only 56 pitches, and his control was as equally impressive, as he tossed 40 strikes and only 16 balls.

Pavano, a former Yankees hurler, struck out eight batters while only throwing 60 pitches — 39 of which were strikes — through the first six innings. He allowed three hits: a single to Melky Cabrera in the third, a seeing-eye single to Hideki Matsui in the fifth and a double to Derek Jeter in the sixth. Pavano didn't allow a run in his first six frames.

In the bottom of the sixth, Twins catcher Joe Mauer staked Pavano to a 1-0 lead with a grounder to left field that scored centerfielder Denard Span.

Trailing, 1-0, in the top of the seventh, the Yankees responded to the Twins' sixth-inning strike.

After Mark Teixeira was retired on a ground ball to third, Rodriguez smacked a line-drive home run over the Metrodome's right-field wall. The blast was A-Rod's second in two games.

Two batters later, Posada deposited a Pavano sinker a few inches over the left-field wall, giving the Yankees a 2-1 lead. Pavano got out of the inning without any additional damage, but did not return to the mound in the eighth.

Rivera

PUNTO TOOK OFF FOR THIRD AND OVERRAN THE BASE. JETER RESPONDED BY THROWING TO POSADA, WHO RELAYED THE BALL TO RODRIGUEZ AT THIRD. RODRIGUEZ TAGGED PUNTO FOR THE CRUCIAL FIRST OUT OF THE EIGHTH.

# GOOD NIGHT, METRODOME

Game 3 of the American League Division Series was the final baseball game played at the Metrodome, and the Yankees etched their place in its history.

Mariano Rivera recorded the final strikeout, fanning Delmon Young in the ninth inning, and Derek Jeter recorded the last out by fielding a Brendan Harris ground ball and tossing it to Mark Teixeira at first base.

On the offensive side, Jorge Posada hit the Metrodome's final home run when he took Twins pitcher Carl Pavano deep in the top of the seventh inning.

With their Game 3 victory, the Yankees finished 5-0 all-time in post-season play at the ballpark.

The Twins began playing their home games within the walls of the downtown Minneapolis dome in 1982, winning championships there in 1987 and 1991. They were scheduled to begin play at the open-air Target Field, also located in downtown Minneapolis, in 2010.

"This was always a tough place to play at," manager Joe Girardi said. "I think it got that reputation during the 1987 World Series and in the 1991 World Series. It's been one of the loudest venues in baseball, and the fans were always into the game."

— Alfred Santasiere III

*Rodriguez (13) and Posada*

Pettitte struck out the first batter in the bottom of the seventh and then was lifted by manager Joe Girardi. Pettitte finished the contest with seven strikeouts over 6 ⅓ innings, giving up three hits and one run.

"People can say whatever they want about the home runs and the big hits, but if you don't pitch well, you aren't going to win," Rodriguez said. "Andy Pettitte is the story tonight. He was fantastic."

Joba Chamberlain replaced Pettitte and surrendered a double to Delmon Young before retiring the next two batters.

Phil Hughes took the mound in the bottom of the eighth for the Yankees and gave up a double to Nick Punto. With Punto on second, Span hit an infield single that Jeter fielded behind second. Punto took off for third and overran the base. Jeter responded by throwing to Posada, who relayed the ball to Rodriguez at third. Rodriguez tagged Punto for the crucial first out of the eighth.

Hughes retired Orlando Cabrera for the second out of the inning.

With Mauer — the American League batting champion — coming to the plate with the game's tying run on first base, Girardi brought in Mariano Rivera. Rivera rewarded the skipper's decision by inducing Mauer to ground out to first base.

In the top of the ninth, the Yankees loaded the bases with consecutive walks by Teixeira, Rodriguez and Matsui. Posada and Robinson Cano followed with back-to-back RBI singles off Twins closer Joe Nathan, expanding the Yankees lead to 4-1.

Rivera pitched a scoreless ninth to close out the series.

---

GAME 3

**NEW YORK YANKEES** 4
**MINNESOTA TWINS** 1

| | 1 2 3 4 5 6 7 8 9 | R | H | E |
|---|---|---|---|---|
| YANKEES | 0 0 0 0 0 0 2 0 2 | 4 | 7 | 0 |
| TWINS | 0 0 0 0 0 1 0 0 0 | 1 | 7 | 0 |

| N.Y. YANKEES | AB | R | H | RBI | BB | SO | LOB | AVG |
|---|---|---|---|---|---|---|---|---|
| Jeter, SS | 4 | 0 | 1 | 0 | 0 | 0 | 1 | .400 |
| Damon, LF | 4 | 0 | 0 | 0 | 0 | 4 | 1 | .083 |
| Gardner, CF | 0 | 0 | 0 | 0 | 0 | 0 | 0 | .000 |
| Teixeira, 1B | 3 | 1 | 0 | 0 | 1 | 1 | 0 | .167 |
| Rodriguez, 3B | 3 | 2 | 1 | 1 | 1 | 1 | 0 | .455 |
| Matsui, DH | 3 | 0 | 1 | 0 | 1 | 2 | 0 | .222 |
| Hairston, PR-DH | 0 | 0 | 0 | 0 | 0 | 0 | 0 | .000 |
| Posada, C | 4 | 1 | 2 | 2 | 0 | 0 | 1 | .364 |
| Cano, 2B | 4 | 0 | 1 | 1 | 0 | 0 | 1 | .167 |
| Swisher, RF | 4 | 0 | 0 | 0 | 0 | 3 | 3 | .083 |
| Cabrera, CF-LF | 4 | 0 | 1 | 0 | 0 | 2 | 3 | .167 |
| TOTALS | 33 | 4 | 7 | 4 | 3 | 13 | 10 | |

BATTING:
2B: Jeter (2, Pavano). HR: Rodriguez (2, 7th inning off Pavano 0 on, 1 out); Posada (1, 7th inning off Pavano 0 on, 2 out). TB: Jeter 2; Rodriguez 4; Matsui; Posada 5; Cano; Cabrera. RBI: Rodriguez (6); Posada 2 (2); Cano (1). 2-out RBI: Posada. Runners left in scoring position, 2 out: Damon; Cabrera 2. GIDP: Cano. Team LOB: 5.

FIELDING:
Outfield assists: Swisher (Cuddyer at 2nd base).

| MINNESOTA | AB | R | H | RBI | BB | SO | LOB | AVG |
|---|---|---|---|---|---|---|---|---|
| Span, CF | 4 | 1 | 2 | 0 | 0 | 1 | 0 | .400 |
| Cabrera, SS | 3 | 0 | 1 | 0 | 1 | 0 | 1 | .154 |
| Mauer, C | 4 | 0 | 1 | 1 | 0 | 1 | 1 | .417 |
| Cuddyer, 1B | 4 | 0 | 2 | 0 | 0 | 1 | 2 | .429 |
| Kubel, DH | 4 | 0 | 0 | 0 | 0 | 3 | 2 | .071 |
| Young, LF | 4 | 0 | 1 | 0 | 0 | 1 | 2 | .083 |
| Harris, 3B | 4 | 0 | 0 | 0 | 0 | 1 | 3 | .250 |
| Morales, DH | 3 | 0 | 0 | 0 | 0 | 2 | 1 | .000 |
| Punto, 2B | 3 | 0 | 1 | 0 | 0 | 0 | 0 | .444 |
| TOTALS | 33 | 1 | 7 | 1 | 1 | 10 | 12 | |

BATTING:
2B: Young (1, Chamberlain); Punto (1, Hughes). TB: Span 2; Mauer; Cuddyer 2; Young 2; Punto 2. RBI: Mauer (1). 2-out RBI: Mauer. Runners left in scoring position, 2 out: Cuddyer; Harris; Morales. Team LOB: 6.

BASERUNNING:
SB: Span (1, 2nd base off Pettitte/Posada).

# 09

## CHAMPIONSHIP SERIES

 YANKEES 4

ANGELS 2

ANGELS **1** YANKEES **4**

# PITCHER ON FIRE

BY KRISTINA M. DODGE

## YANKS TAKE ADVANTAGE OF ANGELS MISCUES BEHIND EIGHT STRONG INNINGS FROM SABATHIA

**F**ans and scouts alike anticipated a speed game — and they got one. But it was the Yankees, not the pesky Angels, calling the shots in a 4-1 Bombers victory that kicked off the first American League Championship Series in the Bronx since 2004.

The Yankees smacked timely hits, capitalized on the mistakes of their West Coast rivals and kept the Angels away from the places they cause the most damage — the basepaths — behind an eight-inning gem from CC Sabathia in Game 1.

"He was able to get ahead and change speeds, he threw some real good changeups, [and] I think he commanded both sides of the plate better than we had seen him before," said Angels manager Mike Scioscia. "He pitched a heck of a game. He obviously is one of the best in our league, and he pitched like it tonight against us."

Having pitched in harsh weather during his time in Cleveland, Sabathia was unaffected by the 45-degree temperature that had some players sporting balaclavas, and his regular-season track record against the Angels in 2009 (0-2 with a 6.08 ERA) had little bearing on his outing.

*Sabathia*

The southpaw gave up just four hits and one free pass and allowed more than one base runner in an inning only once, in the fourth, when designated hitter Vladimir Guerrero doubled and first baseman Kendry Morales singled him home for the Angels' only run. Sabathia held the Angels hitless in his final four innings.

"That's why we got CC," said outfielder Johnny Damon. "To be a workhorse during the season, of course, but to shut down teams in the postseason."

Damon broke out of his 1-for-12 Division Series slump, going 2-for-5 and scoring the first of two runs with the help of an Angels error and some miscommunication.

In the bottom of the first inning, Damon singled down the left-field line to move Derek Jeter from first to third. A wide throw to the middle of the infield from left fielder Juan Rivera — who was charged with a throwing error — allowed Damon to advance to second. Alex Rodriguez followed with a sac fly to score Jeter, and a dropped fly ball between infielders Erick Aybar and Chone Figgins allowed Damon to score, giving the Yankees a 2-0 lead.

The Yankees extended their lead in the sixth inning. With two outs and Jeter at the plate, Angels starting pitcher John Lackey attempted to pick off Melky Cabrera, but threw the ball

JETER SCORED ON A SAC FLY. THEN A DROPPED FLY BALL BETWEEN INFIELDERS AYBAR [ABOVE] AND FIGGINS ALLOWED DAMON TO SCORE, GIVING THE YANKEES A 2-0 LEAD.

out of the reach of Morales. Cabrera moved to second on the throwing error and scored when Jeter singled to centerfielder Torii Hunter, who charged the ball, but couldn't hold on to it for the team's third error of the game.

"We can't count on the Angels making three errors every game," said Sabathia. "That's a really good team, fundamentally, defensively, and it's just one of those days."

After the misplay, reliever Jason Bulger replaced Lackey, who had given up four runs — two of them earned — on nine hits.

By contrast, a sharp Yankees defense robbed the Angels of several opportunities to get on base. In the sixth, Damon made a sliding catch to send former Bomber Bobby Abreu back to the dugout. Sabathia followed by bare-handing a Hunter bunt and firing the ball to a stretching Mark Teixeira for the second out of the inning. With one out and one on in the seventh, Robinson Cano snagged a ball off the bat of Howie Kendrick.

Mariano Rivera entered the game in the ninth inning and walked Hunter before striking out Guerrero and getting Juan Rivera and Morales to fly out for his 39th postseason save.

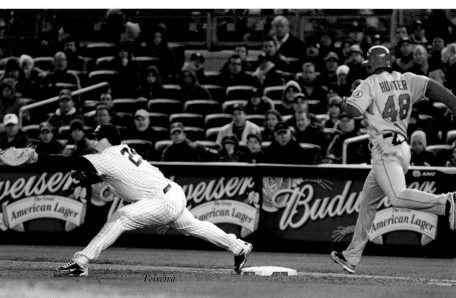

*Teixeira*

# CC STEALS THE SHOW

**W**ith two outs in the top of the seventh, the crowd replaced the standard two-strike clap with a resounding cheer for their hero on the mound — "C-C, C-C, C-C." And CC Sabathia did not disappoint.

The Yankees ace struck out Mike Napoli swinging, and in a rare show of emotion, Sabathia pumped his fist in Tiger Woods-esque jubilation.

"That was a great feeling to have the Stadium rocking and to be chanting my name and to be able to get a strikeout," Sabathia said. "I was pretty pumped up. I don't really show a lot of emotion a lot of times, but it came out of me there."

Sabathia earned the victory by allowing just one run on four hits while striking out seven and walking one in eight innings. With the victory, Sabathia became the first Yankees hurler to win Game 1 of an American League Division Series and Game 1 of the subsequent American League Championship Series since David Wells accomplished the feat in 1998.

— Craig Tapper

| LOS ANGELES | AB | R | H | RBI | BB | SO | LOB | AVG |
|---|---|---|---|---|---|---|---|---|
| Figgins, 3B | 4 | 0 | 0 | 0 | 0 | 1 | 0 | .000 |
| Abreu, RF | 4 | 0 | 0 | 0 | 0 | 2 | 0 | .000 |
| Hunter, CF | 3 | 0 | 1 | 0 | 1 | 0 | 0 | .333 |
| Guerrero, DH | 4 | 1 | 1 | 0 | 0 | 2 | 2 | .250 |
| Rivera, LF | 4 | 0 | 0 | 0 | 0 | 1 | 2 | .000 |
| Morales, 1B | 3 | 0 | 1 | 1 | 1 | 1 | 1 | .333 |
| Kendrick, 2B | 3 | 0 | 1 | 0 | 0 | 0 | 2 | .333 |
| Mathis, C | 2 | 0 | 0 | 0 | 0 | 0 | 1 | .000 |
|  Napoli, PH-C | 1 | 0 | 0 | 0 | 0 | 1 | 1 | .000 |
| Aybar, SS | 3 | 0 | 0 | 0 | 0 | 0 | 0 | .000 |
| TOTALS | 31 | 1 | 4 | 1 | 2 | 8 | 9 | |

| N.Y. YANKEES | AB | R | H | RBI | BB | SO | LOB | AVG |
|---|---|---|---|---|---|---|---|---|
| Jeter, SS | 5 | 1 | 2 | 1 | 0 | 1 | 3 | .400 |
| Damon, LF | 5 | 2 | 2 | 0 | 0 | 0 | 2 | .400 |
|  Gardner, CF | 0 | 0 | 0 | 0 | 0 | 0 | 0 | .000 |
| Teixeira, 1B | 5 | 0 | 1 | 0 | 0 | 2 | 4 | .200 |
| Rodriguez, 3B | 2 | 0 | 1 | 1 | 1 | 1 | 0 | .500 |
| Matsui, DH | 3 | 0 | 2 | 2 | 1 | 0 | 2 | .667 |
| Posada, C | 3 | 0 | 0 | 0 | 1 | 0 | 2 | .000 |
| Cano, 2B | 3 | 0 | 0 | 0 | 0 | 0 | 0 | .000 |
| Swisher, RF | 4 | 0 | 1 | 0 | 0 | 2 | 3 | .250 |
| Cabrera, CF-LF | 2 | 1 | 1 | 0 | 2 | 0 | 0 | .500 |
| TOTALS | 32 | 4 | 10 | 4 | 5 | 6 | 16 | |

## LOS ANGELES ANGELS OF ANAHEIM     1
## NEW YORK YANKEES     4

| | 1 | 2 | 3 | 4 | 5 | 6 | 7 | 8 | 9 | | R | H | E |
|---|---|---|---|---|---|---|---|---|---|---|---|---|---|
| ANGELS | 0 | 0 | 0 | 1 | 0 | 0 | 0 | 0 | 0 | | 1 | 4 | 3 |
| YANKEES | 2 | 0 | 0 | 0 | 1 | 1 | 0 | 0 | X | | 4 | 10 | 0 |

BATTING:

2B: Guerrero (1, Sabathia). TB: Hunter; Guerrero 2; Morales; Kendrick. RBI: Morales (1).
2-out RBI: Morales. Runners left in scoring position, 2 out: Napoli. Team LOB: 5.

FIELDING:

E: Rivera (1, throw); Lackey (1, pickoff); Hunter (1, fielding). Outfield assists: Rivera
(Rodriguez at home).

BATTING:

2B: Damon (1, Lackey); Matsui (1, Lackey). TB: Jeter 2; Damon 3; Teixeira; Rodriguez;
Matsui 3; Swisher; Cabrera. RBI: Jeter; Rodriguez; Matsui 2. 2-out RBI: Jeter; Matsui.
Runners left in scoring position, 2 outs: Jeter; Damon; Teixeira; Matsui; Posada; Swisher
2. SF: Rodriguez. Team LOB: 11.

| LOS ANGELES | IP | H | R | ER | BB | SO | HR | ERA |
|---|---|---|---|---|---|---|---|---|
| Lackey (L, 0-1) | 5⅔ | 9 | 4 | 2 | 3 | 3 | 0 | 3.18 |
| Bulger | 1⅓ | 0 | 0 | 0 | 2 | 2 | 0 | 0.00 |
| Palmer | 1 | 1 | 0 | 0 | 0 | 1 | 0 | 0.00 |

| N.Y. YANKEES | IP | H | R | ER | BB | SO | HR | ERA |
|---|---|---|---|---|---|---|---|---|
| Sabathia (W, 1-0) | 8 | 4 | 1 | 1 | 1 | 7 | 0 | 1.13 |
| Rivera (S, 1) | 1 | 0 | 0 | 0 | 1 | 1 | 0 | 0.00 |

WP: Bulger

HBP: Cano (by Bulger).

Pitches-strikes: Lackey 114-65; Bulger 32-15; Palmer 20-14. Sabathia 113-76; Rivera 17-11.

Ground outs-fly outs: Lackey 4-9; Bulger 1-1; Palmer 2-0. Sabathia 11-6; Rivera 0-2. Batters faced: Lackey 28; Bulger 7; Palmer 4. Sabathia 29; Rivera 4.

Inherited runners-scored: Bulger 1-0.

Umpires: HP: Tim McClelland. 1B: Laz Diaz. 2B: Bill Miller. 3B: Jerry Layne. LF: Fieldin Culbreth. RF: Dale Scott.

Weather: 45 degrees, drizzle. Wind: 10 mph. T: 3:18. Att: 49,688.

# LATE-NIGHT CLASSIC

### BY CRAIG TAPPER

## YANKS WALK OFF (AGAIN) ON 13TH-INNING ERROR

ANGELS **3** YANKEES **4**

**A**fter more than five hours of heart-thumping baseball, the Yankees edged the Angels, 4-3, at home in Game 2 of the American League Championship Series on a Maicer Izturis throwing error that allowed Jerry Hairston Jr. to score from second base.

"A win is a win, regardless," said closer Mariano Rivera, who recorded seven outs in a postseason game for the first time since Game 7 of the 2003 ALCS. "When you win like this, it shows a lot of character, a lot of heart, a lot of determination. That's what we have."

Hairston was honored with the customary pie in the face following the walk-off victory, but the celebration and 2-games-to-none series lead would not have been possible

without another storybook performance from Alex Rodriguez.

With his team trailing, 3-2, in the 11th inning, Rodriguez blasted an opposite-field home run on an 0-2 offering from Angels closer Brian Fuentes, who led the majors in saves during the regular season. It was A-Rod's third game-tying home run of the postseason with all three coming in the seventh inning or later.

"I just kept yelling, 'He did it again! He did it again!'" Yankees first baseman Mark Teixeira said. "I just couldn't believe it."

The extra-innings fireworks overshadowed solid performances by the starting pitchers and the Yankees bullpen.

Rodriguez

Angels starter Joe Saunders yielded two runs on six hits in seven innings while Yankees starter A.J. Burnett sprinkled three hits and two runs over 6 ⅓ innings. Relievers Phil Coke, Joba Chamberlain, Phil Hughes, Rivera, Alfredo Aceves, Damaso Marte and David Robertson then pitched 6 ⅔ innings of five-hit, one-run ball.

The Yankees struck first in the second inning, when Robinson Cano plated Nick Swisher from first with a two-out triple. The Yankees added a run in the third, when Derek Jeter homered to right. The dinger was Jeter's 19th of his career, moving him past Mickey Mantle and Reggie Jackson for sole possession of third place on Major League Baseball's all-time postseason home run list.

The Angels knotted the game in the fifth with two hits, a walk, a hit batsman and a run-scoring wild pitch. After both teams failed to score over the next five innings, the Angels took a 3-2 lead on a Chone Figgins single in the top of the 11th. The hit was the first for Figgins in the postseason, breaking an 0-for-19 slump.

Hairston led off the bottom of the 13th inning with a pinch-hit single off of Ervin Santana, and Brett Gardner sacrificed Hairston to second. After Cano was intentionally walked, Melky Cabrera stepped to the plate with the crowd screaming his name.

Cabrera grounded to the left of Izturis, who threw to second in an attempt to start an inning-ending double play. Izturis' throw was off the mark, and Figgins struggled to pick up the ball near third, allowing Hairston to scamper home with the Yankees' second postseason walk-off win and their 17th walk-off victory of the season.

"I was a little aggressive there," Izturis said. "I'm not scared to be aggressive. Unfortunately, it cost us the game."

Burnett

# 'PEN MIGHTIER
## THAN SWORD

*Chamberlain*

**W**ith the score tied in the seventh inning, A.J. Burnett left the game to an appreciative Yankee Stadium crowd. Little did fans know that their night had only just begun.

Seven Yankees relievers followed, and their collective performance was as good as anyone could ask for. Battling temperatures in the 40s and a steady rain from about the ninth inning through the 11th, the Yanks bullpen allowed just one run over 6 ²/₃ innings.

In the seventh, Joba Chamberlain got a huge out when he whiffed Vladimir Guerrero with the bases loaded. Guerrero, a lifetime .321 hitter, stranded a total of seven runners in scoring position, all with two outs.

Mariano Rivera came in with two outs and two men on in the eighth and got a first-pitch ground-ball out before tossing two scoreless frames. After yielding the go-ahead run in the 11th, Alfredo Aceves induced a key double play to end the inning. And David Robertson pitched 1 ¹/₃ scoreless innings in picking up his second postseason win.

"We have some relievers with some serious guts," Alex Rodriguez said. "A.J. threw the ball extremely well, but you can't say enough about our bullpen. They did a phenomenal job."

— Nathan Maciborski

GAME **2**

| LOS ANGELES | AB | R | H | RBI | BB | SO | LOB | AVG |
|---|---|---|---|---|---|---|---|---|
| Figgins, 3B | 3 | 0 | 1 | 1 | 2 | 1 | 0 | .143 |
| Abreu, RF | 5 | 0 | 0 | 0 | 2 | 2 | 5 | .000 |
| Hunter, CF | 6 | 0 | 2 | 0 | 1 | 1 | 4 | .333 |
| Guerrero, DH | 7 | 0 | 1 | 0 | 0 | 2 | 8 | .182 |
| Morales, 1B | 5 | 0 | 0 | 0 | 0 | 2 | 1 | .125 |
| Rivera, LF | 4 | 0 | 1 | 0 | 0 | 0 | 1 | .125 |
| Willits, PR | 0 | 0 | 0 | 0 | 0 | 0 | 0 | .000 |
| Mathis, C | 2 | 0 | 1 | 0 | 0 | 0 | 1 | .250 |
| Izturis, 2B | 5 | 1 | 1 | 0 | 1 | 0 | 1 | .200 |
| Napoli, C | 3 | 0 | 0 | 0 | 0 | 0 | 1 | .000 |
| Matthews, PH-LF | 2 | 1 | 0 | 0 | 1 | 2 | 4 | .000 |
| Aybar, SS | 5 | 1 | 1 | 1 | 0 | 0 | 2 | .125 |
| TOTALS | 47 | 3 | 8 | 2 | 7 | 10 | 28 | |

**BATTING:**
2B: Hunter (1, Burnett); Mathis (1, Robertson); Izturis (1, Burnett). TB: Figgins; Hunter 3; Guerrero; Rivera; Mathis 2; Izturis 2; Aybar. RBI: Figgins (1); Aybar (1). Runners left in scoring position, 2 out: Guerrero 7; Aybar; Matthews. S: Figgins; Aybar. GIDP: Hunter. Team LOB: 16.

**BASERUNNING:**
SB: Aybar (1, 2nd base off Burnett/Molina).

**FIELDING:**
E: Figgins (1, throw); Izturis (1, throw). DP: 3 (Saunders-Aybar-Morales; Morales-Aybar-Saunders; Izturis-Aybar-Morales).

**LOS ANGELES ANGELS OF ANAHEIM**     **3**
**NEW YORK YANKEES**     **4**

| | 1 | 2 | 3 | 4 | 5 | 6 | 7 | 8 | 9 | 10 | 11 | 12 | 13 | R | H | E |
|---|---|---|---|---|---|---|---|---|---|---|---|---|---|---|---|---|
| ANGELS | 0 | 0 | 0 | 0 | 2 | 0 | 0 | 0 | 0 | 0 | 1 | 0 | 0 | 3 | 8 | 2 |
| YANKEES | 0 | 1 | 1 | 0 | 0 | 0 | 0 | 0 | 0 | 0 | 1 | 0 | 1 | 4 | 13 | 3 |

| N.Y. YANKEES | AB | R | H | RBI | BB | SO | LOB | AVG |
|---|---|---|---|---|---|---|---|---|
| Jeter, SS | 5 | 1 | 1 | 1 | 1 | 1 | 3 | .300 |
| Damon, LF | 6 | 0 | 2 | 0 | 0 | 1 | 3 | .364 |
| Teixeira, 1B | 5 | 0 | 0 | 0 | 1 | 1 | 3 | .100 |
| Rodriguez, 3B | 6 | 1 | 1 | 1 | 0 | 0 | 5 | .250 |
| Matsui, DH | 4 | 0 | 1 | 0 | 0 | 0 | 1 | .429 |
| Guzman, PR-DH | 1 | 0 | 0 | 0 | 0 | 1 | 0 | .000 |
| Hairston, PH-DH | 1 | 1 | 1 | 0 | 0 | 0 | 0 | 1.000 |
| Swisher, RF | 2 | 1 | 1 | 0 | 1 | 0 | 0 | .333 |
| Gardner, PR-CF | 2 | 0 | 1 | 0 | 0 | 0 | 0 | .500 |
| Cano, 2B | 5 | 0 | 1 | 1 | 1 | 0 | 3 | .125 |
| Cabrera, CF-RF | 6 | 0 | 2 | 0 | 0 | 3 | 1 | .375 |
| Molina, C | 2 | 0 | 1 | 0 | 0 | 1 | 0 | .500 |
| Posada, PH-C | 3 | 0 | 1 | 0 | 0 | 0 | 1 | .167 |
| TOTALS | 48 | 4 | 13 | 3 | 4 | 8 | 20 | |

**BATTING:**

3B: Cano (1, Saunders). HR: Jeter (1, 3rd inning off Saunders, 0 on, 1 out); Rodriguez (1, 11th inning off Fuentes, 0 on, 0 out). TB: Jeter 4; Damon 2; Rodriguez 4; Matsui; Hairston; Swisher; Gardner; Cano 3; Cabrera 2; Molina; Posada. RBI: Jeter (2); Rodriguez (2); Cano (1). 2-out RBI: Cano. Runners left in scoring position, 2 out: Damon; Teixeira; Rodriguez 2; Cano 2; Cabrera. S: Gardner. GIDP: Jeter; Matsui; Cano. Team LOB: 12.

**FIELDING:**

E: Jeter (1, fielding); Cano 2 (fielding, fielding). DP: (Rodriguez-Cano-Teixeira).

| LOS ANGELES | IP | H | R | ER | BB | SO | HR | ERA |
|---|---|---|---|---|---|---|---|---|
| Saunders | 7 | 6 | 2 | 2 | 1 | 5 | 1 | 2.57 |
| Jepsen | 2 | 2 | 0 | 0 | 1 | 0 | 0 | 0.00 |
| Oliver | 1 | 1 | 0 | 0 | 1 | 0 | 0 | 0.00 |
| Fuentes (BS, 1) | 1 | 1 | 1 | 1 | 0 | 1 | 1 | 9.00 |
| Santana (L, 0-1) | 1⅓ | 3 | 1 | 0 | 2 | 1 | 0 | 0.00 |

| N.Y. YANKEES | IP | H | R | ER | BB | SO | HR | ERA |
|---|---|---|---|---|---|---|---|---|
| Burnett | 6⅓ | 3 | 2 | 2 | 2 | 4 | 0 | 2.84 |
| Coke | ⅓ | 0 | 0 | 0 | 1 | 1 | 0 | 0.00 |
| Chamberlain | ⅓ | 1 | 0 | 0 | 0 | 1 | 0 | 0.00 |
| Hughes | ⅔ | 1 | 0 | 0 | 0 | 1 | 0 | 0.00 |
| Rivera | 2⅓ | 1 | 0 | 0 | 0 | 2 | 0 | 0.00 |
| Aceves | 1⅓ | 1 | 1 | 1 | 2 | 0 | 0 | 6.75 |
| Marte | ⅓ | 0 | 0 | 0 | 0 | 0 | 0 | 0.00 |
| Robertson (W, 1-0) | 1⅓ | 1 | 0 | 0 | 2 | 1 | 0 | 0.00 |

WP: Burnett. IBB: Jeter (by Oliver); Cano (by Santana); Abreu (by Aceves); Izturis (by Robertson); Abreu (by Robertson). HBP: Figgins (by Burnett); Morales (by Burnett).

Pitches-strikes: Saunders 105-57; Jepsen 28-17; Oliver 23-11; Fuentes 16-13; Santana 30-15. Burnett 114-75; Coke 11-5; Chamberlain 10-7; Hughes 9-8; Rivera 25-17; Aceves 24-13; Marte 4-3; Robertson 33-17. Ground outs-fly outs: Saunders 11-5; Jepsen 5-0; Oliver 2-1; Fuentes 2-0; Santana 2-1. Burnett 6-9; Coke 0-0; Chamberlain 0-0; Hughes 0-1; Rivera 2-3; Aceves 3-1; Marte 1-0; Robertson 3-0. Batters Faced: Saunders 26; Jepsen 8; Oliver 5; Fuentes 4; Santana 10. Burnett 27; Coke 2; Chamberlain 2; Hughes 4; Rivera 8; Aceves 6; Marte 1; Robertson 8. Inherited runners-scored: Coke 1-0; Chamberlain 2-0; Rivera 2-0.

Umpires: HP: Laz Diaz. 1B: Bill Miller. 2B: Jerry Layne. 3B: Fieldin Culbreth. LF: Dale Scott. RF: Tim McClelland.

Weather: 47 degrees, cloudy. Wind: 11 mph. T: 5:10 Att: 49,922.

 **2009 CHAMPIONSHIP SERIES**
GAME 3, OCT. 19, 2009

# TOUGH LOSS

BY ALFRED SANTASIERE III

DESPITE FOUR HOMERS, YANKS FALL TO ANGELS IN EXTRA INNINGS

YANKEES 4 ANGELS 5

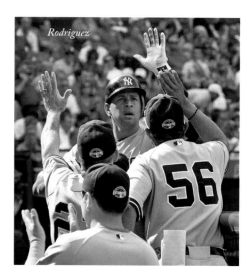
*Rodriguez*

The Angels overcame a deficit of at least three runs for the 16th time in 2009 when they beat the Yankees, 5-4, in 11 innings at home in Game 3 of the American League Championship Series.

The 4-hour, 21-minute affair had many twists and turns, much like the rest of the postseason for the Yankees.

The Bombers jumped to a quick lead in the first inning, when Derek Jeter drove Jered Weaver's third pitch over the left-field wall. Alex Rodriguez followed in the fourth with a solo home run that cleared both bullpens in left, and Johnny Damon hit a solo shot down the right-field line in the fifth, putting the Bombers ahead, 3-0. It was the first time in 35 regular- and postseason starts that Weaver allowed more than two home runs.

Angels second baseman Howie Kendrick homered off of Andy Pettitte in the fifth, narrowing the Yanks' lead to 3-1.

In the bottom of the sixth, Angels right fielder Bobby Abreu singled and designated hitter Vladimir Guerrero drove him in with a two-out, two-run homer, tying the game, 3-3.

After Pettitte retired Kendry Morales for the first out in the seventh, manager Joe Girardi gave the ball to Joba Chamberlain. Kendrick drove Chamberlain's first offering off the right-field wall for a triple, and the next batter, pinch-

# YANKEES FANS
## MAKE THEMSELVES AT HOME WHILE TEAM'S ON THE ROAD

The smell of hot dogs and all the typical sounds of a Yankees home game filled Yankee Stadium as 5,669 Bombers fans (and one Mets fan, who was heckled incessantly) gathered to watch Game 3 on the center-field video board.

"This is amazing, this idea," said Bronx resident Sylvia Gonzalez. "I hope they do this again."

Chants of "Let's go Yan-kees!" were common as fans reacted to each pitch as if the team were playing on the field in front of them, high-fiving one another after big plays such as Derek Jeter's leadoff home run.

The Yankees made portions of the Field Level and the Great Hall available for fans to watch the broadcast.

"We wanted to provide a place for our fans to come together to cheer for our team even if the game itself is taking place across the country," said Yankees co-chairperson/managing general partner Hal Steinbrenner. "This is a way of saying thank you for their continued support."

"I'm so happy that [the Yankees] thought it was a good opportunity for people, particularly those who haven't seen the Stadium yet, to come out and be one big Bronx happy family," said Bronx Borough President Ruben Diaz Jr.

— **Nathan Maciborski**

IN THE BOTTOM OF THE SIXTH, ABREU SINGLED AND GUERRERO DROVE HIM IN WITH A TWO-OUT, TWO-RUN HOMER OFF PETTITTE, TYING THE GAME, 3-3.

*Pettitte*

*Abreu*

hitter Maicer Izturis, scored him on a sac fly to right, putting the Angels ahead, 4-3.

With one out in the top of the eighth inning and Angels reliever Kevin Jepsen on the mound, Jorge Posada tied the game with a solo home run.

Abreu responded with a leadoff double to center off Phil Coke in the eighth, but he was thrown out rounding second by a strong relay from Melky Cabrera to Jeter, who threw to Mark Teixeira at second.

In the bottom of the 10th, Phil Hughes gave up a leadoff double to Angels catcher Jeff Mathis, prompting Girardi to bring in Mariano Rivera.

Rivera first faced Erick Aybar, who placed a bunt between the mound and third base. Rivera fielded the ball and went to third, but tossed it out of Rodriguez' reach. Rivera's miscue put Aybar on first and Mathis on third with no outs.

Rivera then induced three ground-ball outs to Teixeira at first base, preventing further, if not imminent, disaster.

"They kept me pretty busy over there," Teixeira said after the game. "That was an incredible job by Mo. He never ceases to amaze me."

In the bottom of the 11th, David Robertson retired the first two Angels, then was replaced by Alfredo Aceves.

Aceves gave up a single to Kendrick. Mathis followed with a drive to the left-center field wall, scoring Kendrick for the game-winning run and shortening the Yankees' series lead to 2 games to 1.

"There was a lot of great baseball on that field this afternoon," Angels manager Mike Scioscia said. "There were a lot of twists and turns, and both teams played a terrific game. We just got it done at the end."

# DEFENSIVE DANDY

**P**roducing at the plate isn't the only way to contribute. Just ask Mark Teixeira.

Teixeira's glovework and defensive savvy — which earned the first baseman Gold Glove Awards in 2005, 2006 and 2009 — were on display during Game 3. In the 10th, Teixeira made three key defensive plays to keep the Angels from pushing across the winning run: a diving stop to hold the winning run at third, a strong throw to force out the winning run at the plate and a smooth pickup on a grounder to end the inning.

"There's a lot of ways that you can win a ballgame," said Yankees manager Joe Girardi. "It just doesn't always have to be with your bat. Tex has saved us defensively during this series a number of times."

Earlier, Teixeira's defense helped produce a baseball oddity. Angels right fielder Bobby Abreu led off the eighth inning with a double to right-center, but rounded the bag too far before slamming on the brakes. Melky Cabrera fielded the ball and fired it to Derek Jeter, who alertly threw the ball to Teixeira. Teixeira, covering at second base, applied the tag on Abreu. The 8-6-3 putout was just the second such putout in postseason history.

— Craig Tapper

**GAME 3**

| N.Y. YANKEES | AB | R | H | RBI | BB | SO | LOB | AVG |
|---|---|---|---|---|---|---|---|---|
| Jeter, SS | 6 | 1 | 1 | 1 | 0 | 1 | 2 | .250 |
| Damon, LF | 5 | 1 | 1 | 1 | 0 | 1 | 0 | .313 |
| Rivera, P | 0 | 0 | 0 | 0 | 0 | 0 | 0 | .000 |
| Cervelli, PH | 1 | 0 | 0 | 0 | 0 | 1 | 0 | .000 |
| Robertson, P | 0 | 0 | 0 | 0 | 0 | 0 | 0 | .000 |
| Aceves, P | 0 | 0 | 0 | 0 | 0 | 0 | 0 | .000 |
| Teixeira, 1B | 3 | 0 | 0 | 0 | 2 | 2 | 0 | .077 |
| Rodriguez, 3B | 4 | 1 | 1 | 1 | 1 | 0 | 2 | .250 |
| Matsui, DH | 2 | 0 | 1 | 0 | 2 | 1 | 1 | .444 |
| Gardner, PR-DH | 0 | 0 | 0 | 0 | 0 | 0 | 0 | .500 |
| Hairston, PH-DH-LF | 1 | 0 | 0 | 0 | 0 | 1 | 1 | .500 |
| Posada, C | 4 | 1 | 2 | 1 | 1 | 2 | 0 | .300 |
| Cano, 2B | 5 | 0 | 2 | 0 | 0 | 4 | 4 | .231 |
| Swisher, RF | 4 | 0 | 0 | 0 | 1 | 3 | 5 | .200 |
| Cabrera, CF | 5 | 0 | 0 | 0 | 0 | 1 | 7 | .231 |
| TOTALS | 40 | 4 | 8 | 4 | 7 | 13 | 22 | |

**BATTING:**

HR: Jeter (2, 1st inning off Weaver, 0 on, 0 out); Rodriguez (2, 4th inning off Weaver, 0 on, 0 out); Damon (1, 5th inning off Weaver, 0 on, 1 out); Posada (1, off Jepsen, 0 on, 1 out). TB: Jeter 4; Damon 4; Rodriguez 4; Matsui; Posada 5; Cano 2. RBI: Jeter (3); Damon (1); Rodriguez (3); Posada (1). Runners left in scoring position, 2 out: Jeter; Cabrera 2. Team LOB: 10.

**BASERUNNING:**

CS: Gardner (1, 2nd base by Jepsen/Mathis).

**FIELDING:**

Outfield assists: Cabrera (Abreu at 3rd base). DP: 2 (Jeter-Teixeira; Jeter-Cano-Teixeira). Pickoffs: Pettitte (Hunter at 1st base).

**NEW YORK YANKEES**     4
**LOS ANGELES ANGELS OF ANAHEIM**     5

| | 1 | 2 | 3 | 4 | 5 | 6 | 7 | 8 | 9 | 10 | 11 | R | H | E |
|---|---|---|---|---|---|---|---|---|---|---|---|---|---|---|
| YANKEES | 1 | 0 | 0 | 1 | 1 | 0 | 0 | 1 | 0 | 0 | 0 | 4 | 8 | 0 |
| ANGELS | 0 | 0 | 0 | 0 | 1 | 2 | 1 | 0 | 0 | 0 | 1 | 5 | 13 | 0 |

| LOS ANGELES | AB | R | H | RBI | BB | SO | LOB | AVG |
|---|---|---|---|---|---|---|---|---|
| Figgins, 3B | 5 | 0 | 1 | 0 | 0 | 0 | 4 | .167 |
| Abreu, RF | 4 | 1 | 2 | 0 | 1 | 0 | 1 | .154 |
| Hunter, CF | 5 | 0 | 1 | 0 | 0 | 1 | 5 | .286 |
| Guerrero, DH | 4 | 1 | 2 | 2 | 1 | 0 | 3 | .267 |
| Rivera, LF | 5 | 0 | 0 | 0 | 0 | 0 | 2 | .077 |
| Morales, 1B | 5 | 0 | 0 | 0 | 0 | 1 | 1 | .077 |
| Kendrick, 2B | 5 | 3 | 3 | 1 | 0 | 0 | 0 | .500 |
| Napoli, C | 2 | 0 | 0 | 0 | 0 | 1 | 0 | .000 |
| Izturis, PH | 0 | 0 | 0 | 1 | 0 | 0 | 0 | .200 |
| Mathis, C | 2 | 0 | 2 | 1 | 0 | 0 | 0 | .500 |
| Aybar, SS | 3 | 0 | 2 | 0 | 0 | 0 | 0 | .273 |
| TOTALS | 40 | 5 | 13 | 5 | 2 | 3 | 16 | |

BATTING:
2B: Abreu (1, Coke); Mathis 2 (3, Hughes, Aceves); Aybar (1, Chamberlain). 3B: Kendrick (1, Chamberlain). HR: Kendrick (1, 5th inning off Pettitte, 0 on, 1 out). Guerrero (1, 6th inning off Pettitte, 1 on, 2 out). TB: Figgins; Abreu 3; Hunter; Guerrero 5; Kendrick 8; Mathis 4; Aybar 3. RBI: Guerrero 2 (2); Kendrick (1); Izturis (1); Mathis (1). 2-out RBI: Guerrero 2; Mathis. Runners left in scoring position, 2 out: Figgins 2; Guerrero 2. S: Aybar. SF: Izturis. GIDP: Hunter; Morales. Team LOB: 7.

BASERUNNING:
SB: Aybar (2, 2nd base off Pettitte/Posada). CS: Hunter (1, 2nd base by Pettitte/Teixeira/Cano). PO: Hunter (1st base by Pettitte).

| N.Y. YANKEES | IP | H | R | ER | BB | SO | HR | ERA |
|---|---|---|---|---|---|---|---|---|
| Pettitte | 6⅓ | 7 | 3 | 3 | 1 | 2 | 2 | 4.26 |
| Chamberlain | ⅓ | 2 | 1 | 1 | 0 | 0 | 0 | 13.50 |
| Marte | ⅓ | 0 | 0 | 0 | 0 | 0 | 0 | 0.00 |
| Coke | ⅓ | 1 | 0 | 0 | 0 | 0 | 0 | 0.00 |
| Hughes | 1⅓ | 1 | 0 | 0 | 0 | 1 | 0 | 0.00 |
| Rivera | 1 | 0 | 0 | 0 | 1 | 0 | 0 | 0.00 |
| Robertson | ⅔ | 0 | 0 | 0 | 0 | 0 | 0 | 0.00 |
| Aceves (L, 0-1) | 0 | 2 | 1 | 1 | 0 | 0 | 0 | 13.50 |

| LOS ANGELES | IP | H | R | ER | BB | SO | HR | ERA |
|---|---|---|---|---|---|---|---|---|
| Weaver | 5 | 5 | 3 | 3 | 3 | 4 | 3 | 5.40 |
| Oliver | 1⅓ | 1 | 0 | 0 | 1 | 3 | 0 | 0.00 |
| Jepsen | 1⅓ | 2 | 1 | 1 | 2 | 1 | 1 | 2.70 |
| Fuentes | 1 | 0 | 0 | 0 | 1 | 2 | 0 | 4.50 |
| Bulger | 1 | 0 | 0 | 0 | 0 | 2 | 0 | 0.00 |
| Santana (W, 1-1) | 1 | 0 | 0 | 0 | 1 | 0 | 0 | 0.00 |

IBB: Abreu (by Rivera); Rodriguez (Fuentes).
Pitches-strikes: Pettitte 95-59; Chamberlain 10-6; Marte 1-1; Coke 3-2; Hughes 19-15; Rivera 17-10. Robertson 11-6; Aceves 7-3; Weaver 95-59; Oliver 28-17; Jepsen 31-15; Fuentes 13-8; Bulger 13-8; Santana 9-6.

Ground outs-fly outs: Pettitte 7-9; Chamberlain 0-1; Marte 0-1; Coke 0-0; Hughes 2-2; Rivera 3-0; Robertson 1-1; Aceves 0-0. Weaver 4-7; Oliver 0-2; Jepsen 2-0; Fuentes 1-0; Bulger 1-0; Santana 1-1.

Batters faced: Pettitte 24; Chamberlain 3; Marte 1; Coke 1; Hughes 6; Rivera 5; Robertson 2; Aceves 2. Weaver 23; Oliver 7; Jepsen 7; Fuentes 4; Bulger 3; Santana 3.
Inherited runners-scored: Marte 1-0; Rivera 1-0. Jepsen 1-0.

Umpires: HP: Bill Miller. 1B: Jerry Layne. 2B: Fieldin Culbreth. 3B: Dale Scott. LF: Tim McClelland. RF: Laz Diaz.

Weather: 73 degrees, cloudy. Wind: 5 mph. T: 4:21. Att: 44,911.

# IN COMMAND

BY ALFRED SANTASIERE III

SABATHIA STELLAR ON THREE DAYS' REST AND BATS
HOT AS YANKS PUMMEL ANGELS, 10-1

**2009 CHAMPIONSHIP SERIES**
GAME 4, OCT. 20, 2009

**YANKEES 10 ANGELS 1**

The Angels were in need of some relief. Already trailing, 3-0, in Game 4 of the American League Championship Series and 2 games to 1 in the best-of-seven series, the Angels pulled their starting pitcher, Scott Kazmir, after he allowed a leadoff single to Mark Teixeira in the top of the fifth inning.

But the Angels didn't get the relief they were looking for.

Alex Rodriguez hit Jason Bulger's second offering over the left-field wall. The home run was A-Rod's third in three games, his fifth of the 2009 postseason, and it gave the Yankees a 5-0 lead en route to a 10-1 victory.

"Alex has been as good as anyone I ever played alongside in the postseason," said manager Joe Girardi. "I don't remember any player on our great clubs that put up the

> ## "I feel pretty locked in. I never doubted that I could pitch well on this stage, but I'm glad it's going this well."
>
> ### — SABATHIA

numbers Alex has in back-to-back series. He's been a great player for a long time, but he's in a zone right now."

CC Sabathia took the ball for the Yankees on three days' rest, and he limited the Angels to one run and five hits over eight innings. In doing so, he became the seventh Yankees pitcher to record three wins in a single postseason.

"I feel pretty locked in," Sabathia said. "I never doubted that I could pitch well on this stage, but I'm glad it's going this well."

The Yankees broke through against Kazmir in the top of the fourth. Rodriguez led off with a single, and Jorge Posada moved him to third with a double. Robinson Cano scored Rodriguez with a ground ball to second.

Two batters later, Melky Cabrera hit a ground ball between short and third that plated Posada and Cano, giving the Yankees a 3-0 lead.

Sabathia sailed through the first four innings,

throwing only 38 pitches while allowing no runs and only an infield hit.

In the bottom of the fifth, Sabathia hit choppy water for the first time.

With one out, Angels first baseman Kendry Morales hit a solo home run to left-center field, closing the Yankees lead to 5-1. Mike Napoli singled past a diving A-Rod, and Erick Aybar advanced him to second with a single to centerfield.

Sabathia got out of the inning without giving up any additional runs, retiring Chone Figgins and Bobby Abreu.

Angels reliever Ervin Santana hit Nick Swisher to start the eighth inning. Girardi replaced Swisher with pinch-runner Brett Gardner, who was caught stealing for the first out.

After Santana walked Cabrera, Angels skipper Mike Scioscia pulled Santana from the game in favor of Matt Palmer.

Palmer quickly retired Derek Jeter on a ground ball for the second out of the inning, but Johnny Damon followed with his second home run in as many nights. The two-run shot gave the Yankees a 7-1 lead.

Sabathia regained his dominant form in the late innings, sitting down the last eight Angels he faced.

"He was spectacular again," Girardi said. "To be able to shut this club down the way he did is no easy feat. They have a very dangerous lineup, and CC just kept getting outs for us."

Cabrera capped the scoring in the top of the ninth with a two-run double that put the Yankees ahead, 10-1, and Chad Gaudin closed out the Angels in the bottom of the frame.

*Rodriguez*

> "He was spectacular again. To be able to shut this club down the way he did is no easy feat. They have a very dangerous lineup, and CC just kept getting outs for us."
> — GIRARDI

# CRUISE CONTROL

**CC** Sabathia walked off the mound in the bottom of the seventh after disposing the Angels in 12 pitches — strikeout, strikeout, ground ball to first — prompting TV announcer Tim McCarver to remark, "I think this was his strongest inning."

Then came the eighth. Mixing in two sliders among a steady stream of perfectly placed mid-90s fastballs, Sabathia needed just *nine* pitches to retire the side — groundout, strikeout, groundout.

At a time of year when most pitchers would be running on fumes, Sabathia's late-inning performances in his two American League Championship Series starts were the definition of dominance. The hefty lefty's numbers in innings 6 through 8: 20 batters faced, one hit, two walks, six strikeouts and one very happy manager.

"I don't think you can say enough about what he's done so far in this series," Joe Girardi said. "For him not to throw a ton of pitches in eight innings, he gave us what we needed."

— Nathan Maciborski

EVEN THOUGH THE GAME PROVIDED SEVERAL CONFUSING PLAYS ON THE BASEPATHS, THE YANKEES WERE ABLE TO COME AWAY WITH THE VICTORY.

| ALCS 2009 | GAME | 4 |
| --- | --- | --- |

| NEW YORK YANKEES | 10 |
| --- | --- |
| LOS ANGELES ANGELS OF ANAHEIM | 1 |

| | 1 | 2 | 3 | 4 | 5 | 6 | 7 | 8 | 9 | | R | H | E |
| --- | --- | --- | --- | --- | --- | --- | --- | --- | --- | --- | --- | --- | --- |
| YANKEES | 0 | 0 | 0 | 3 | 2 | 0 | 0 | 2 | 3 | | 10 | 13 | 0 |
| ANGELS | 0 | 0 | 0 | 0 | 1 | 0 | 0 | 0 | 0 | | 1 | 5 | 1 |

| N.Y. YANKEES | AB | R | H | RBI | BB | SO | LOB | AVG |
| --- | --- | --- | --- | --- | --- | --- | --- | --- |
| Jeter, SS | 5 | 0 | 2 | 0 | 1 | 0 | 3 | .286 |
| Damon, LF | 5 | 1 | 1 | 2 | 0 | 0 | 5 | .286 |
| Teixeira, 1B | 5 | 1 | 1 | 0 | 0 | 2 | 2 | .111 |
| Rodriguez, 3B | 4 | 3 | 3 | 2 | 1 | 1 | 1 | .375 |
| Posada, C | 3 | 1 | 1 | 0 | 2 | 1 | 0 | .308 |
| Matsui, DH | 5 | 0 | 0 | 0 | 0 | 3 | 5 | .286 |
| Cano, 2B | 4 | 2 | 1 | 1 | 1 | 1 | 3 | .235 |
| Swisher, RF | 2 | 0 | 0 | 0 | 1 | 0 | 4 | .167 |
| Gardner, PR-CF | 1 | 1 | 1 | 0 | 0 | 0 | 0 | .667 |
| Cabrera, CF-RF | 4 | 1 | 3 | 4 | 1 | 0 | 2 | .353 |
| TOTALS | 38 | 10 | 13 | 9 | 7 | 8 | 25 | |

**BATTING:**

2B: Rodriguez (1, Palmer); Posada (1, Kazmir); Cano (1, Oliver); Cabrera (1, Palmer). HR: Rodriguez (3, 5th inning off Bulger, 1 on, 0 out); Damon (2, 8th inning off Palmer, 1 on, 2 out). TB: Jeter 2; Damon 4; Teixeira; Rodriguez 7; Posada 2; Cano 2; Gardner; Cabrera 4. RBI: Damon 2 (3); Rodriguez 2 (5); Cano (2); Cabrera 4 (4). 2-out RBI: Damon 2; Cabrera 2. Runners left in scoring position, 2 out: Jeter; Teixeira; Rodriguez; Swisher; Cabrera. Team LOB: 9.

**BASERUNNING:**

SB: Rodriguez (1, 2nd base off Kazmir/Napoli); Posada (1, 2nd base off Oliver/Napoli). CS: Jeter (1, 2nd base by Kazmir/Morales/Aybar); Gardner (2, 2nd base by Santana/Napoli). PO: Jeter (1st base by Kazmir).

**FIELDING:**

DP: (Jeter-Teixeira).

| LOS ANGELES | AB | R | H | RBI | BB | SO | LOB | AVG |
|---|---|---|---|---|---|---|---|---|
| Figgins, 3B | 4 | 0 | 0 | 0 | 0 | 0 | 2 | .125 |
| Abreu, RF | 3 | 0 | 0 | 0 | 1 | 2 | 2 | .125 |
| Hunter, CF | 3 | 0 | 0 | 0 | 1 | 1 | 1 | .235 |
| Guerrero, DH | 4 | 0 | 1 | 0 | 0 | 0 | 1 | .263 |
| Rivera, LF | 4 | 0 | 1 | 0 | 0 | 0 | 2 | .118 |
| Kendrick, 2B | 3 | 0 | 0 | 0 | 0 | 0 | 2 | .364 |
| Matthews, PH | 1 | 0 | 0 | 0 | 0 | 0 | 0 | .000 |
| Morales, 1B | 3 | 1 | 1 | 1 | 0 | 1 | 1 | .125 |
| Napoli, C | 3 | 0 | 1 | 0 | 0 | 1 | 1 | .111 |
| Aybar, SS | 3 | 0 | 1 | 0 | 0 | 0 | 0 | .286 |
| TOTALS | 31 | 1 | 5 | 1 | 2 | 5 | 12 | |

**BATTING:**

HR: Morales (1, 5th inning off Sabathia 0 on, 1 out). TB: Guerrero; Rivera; Morales 4;
Napoli; Aybar. RBI: Morales (2). Runners left in scoring position, 2 out: Abreu; Kendrick;
Napoli. GIDP: Rivera. Team LOB: 5.

**FIELDING:**

E: Abreu (1, throw). Outfield assists: Hunter (Swisher at 3rd base). DP: (Hunter-Morales-
Figgins). Pickoffs: Kazmir (Jeter at 1st base).

| N.Y. YANKEES | IP | H | R | ER | BB | SO | HR | ERA |
|---|---|---|---|---|---|---|---|---|
| Sabathia (W, 2-0) | 8 | 5 | 1 | 1 | 2 | 5 | 1 | 1.13 |
| Gaudin | 1 | 0 | 0 | 0 | 0 | 0 | 0 | 0.00 |

| LOS ANGELES | IP | H | R | ER | BB | SO | HR | ERA |
|---|---|---|---|---|---|---|---|---|
| Kazmir (L, 0-1) | 4 | 6 | 4 | 4 | 4 | 3 | 0 | 9.00 |
| Bulger | 0 | 1 | 1 | 1 | 1 | 0 | 1 | 3.86 |
| Oliver | 1 | 1 | 0 | 0 | 0 | 1 | 0 | 0.00 |
| Santana | 2⅓ | 1 | 1 | 1 | 1 | 3 | 0 | 1.93 |
| Palmer | 1⅔ | 4 | 4 | 4 | 1 | 1 | 1 | 13.50 |

Kazmir pitched to one batter in the 5th.

WP: Kazmir. HBP: Swisher (by Santana).
Pitches-strikes: Sabathia 101-69; Gaudin 13-9. Kazmir 89-49; Bulger 7-3; Oliver 11-8;
Santana 36-23; Palmer 27-16.

Ground outs-fly outs: Sabathia 14-5; Gaudin 1-2. Kazmir 2-5; Bulger 0-0; Oliver 2-0; Santana
3-0; Palmer 2-2.

Batters Faced: Sabathia 30; Gaudin 3. Kazmir 21; Bulger 2; Oliver 4; Santana 9; Palmer 10.
Inherited runners-scored:  Bulger 1-1; Oliver 1-0; Palmer 1-1.

Umpires:  HP: Jerry Layne. 1B: Fieldin Culbreth. 2B: Dale Scott. 3B: Tim McClelland. LF:
Laz Diaz. RF: Bill Miller.

Weather: 73 degrees, sunny. Wind: 6 mph. T: 3:38 Att: 45,160.

# BATTLE
## TO THE FINISH

BY ALFRED SANTASIERE III

### AFTER SEVENTH-INNING, SIX-RUN SURGE, YANKS FALL TO ANGELS, 7-6

YANKEES  6 ANGELS  7

The Angels defeated the Yankees, 7-6, in a seesaw American League Championship Series Game 5 at Angel Stadium of Anaheim. With the win, the Angels narrowed the Yankees' series lead to 3 games to 2, sending the teams back to the Bronx.

The Angels took a sizeable jump in the first inning against Yankees righthander A.J. Burnett. Burnett allowed the Angels' first four batters

to reach base and score before getting second baseman Maicer Izturis to fly out to right field for the first out of the inning. The next batter, left fielder Juan Rivera, grounded into a double play, and Burnett escaped the first inning without any further damage. He settled in and gave up only three hits while not surrendering any runs over the next five frames.

Armed with the early 4-0 lead, Angels starting

pitcher John Lackey cruised through the first five innings of the game. After surrendering back-to-back singles to Derek Jeter and Johnny Damon at the start of the game, Lackey scattered three more hits and didn't allow a run through the sixth.

In the top of the seventh, Lackey gave up a one-out double to Melky Cabrera before walking Jorge Posada and Jeter. Lackey retired Damon for the second out, and Angels manager Mike Scioscia pulled him from the game in favor of Darren Oliver.

Mark Teixeira swatted Oliver's first offering to deep left-center for a three-run double. After an intentional walk to Alex Rodriguez, Hideki Matsui singled to right-center, moving A-Rod to second, scoring Teixeira and tying the game at four.

"I was just looking for something out over the plate," Teixeira said. "I got a slider in the

*Lackey*

middle of the plate and put a good swing on it."

Following Matsui's game-tying single, Scioscia replaced Oliver on the mound with Kevin Jepsen.

Jepsen was unable to keep the game knotted at four, giving up a triple to Robinson Cano that scored Rodriguez and Matsui. Cano's three-base hit gave the Yankees a 6-4 advantage.

The Yankees' lead would be short-lived.

Angels catcher Jeff Mathis led off the bottom of the seventh with a single, and Erick Aybar walked.

With two runners on the basepaths and no outs, Joe Girardi signaled to the bullpen, bringing in Damaso Marte for Burnett.

"I know I did my best out there and left it on the field for my team," Burnett said. "Unfortunately, in the seventh inning, I just couldn't get it started."

Chone Figgins laid down a sacrifice bunt that moved Mathis to third and Aybar to second, and Bobby Abreu scored Mathis and moved

# BAT HAPPY

*Teixeira*

For six innings, the Yankees offense could muster only five hits off of Angels starter John Lackey. But in the seventh frame, the Bombers broke through in a big way, turning a 4-0 deficit into a 6-4 lead.

"These guys — bam-bam — with the good offense that they have, they came back," said Angels centerfielder Torii Hunter. "When they got the sixth run, man, I was out there deflated, you know, and [ticked] off."

The rally featured a Mark Teixeira bases-clearing double, a Hideki Matsui run-scoring single and a Robinson Cano two-run triple.

The Yankees' six-run seventh inning was their biggest postseason outburst since Game 4 of the 2003 American League Division Series, when they scored six runs in the fourth inning against the Twins. Game 5 also marked the first time that the Yanks scored six runs in a postseason inning all with two outs.

— Craig Tapper

HUNTER HAD TWO
HITS, TWO RUNS, TWO
RBI AND TWO WALKS
TO LEAD THE ANGELS TO
VICTORY.

*Cano*

ALDS 2009

GAME 5

NEW YORK YANKEES     6
LOS ANGELES ANGELS OF ANAHEIM     7

|  | 1 | 2 | 3 | 4 | 5 | 6 | 7 | 8 | 9 | R | H | E |
|---|---|---|---|---|---|---|---|---|---|---|---|---|
| YANKEES | 0 | 0 | 0 | 0 | 0 | 0 | 6 | 0 | 0 | 6 | 9 | 0 |
| ANGELS | 4 | 0 | 0 | 0 | 0 | 0 | 3 | 0 | X | 7 | 12 | 0 |

| N.Y. YANKEES | AB | R | H | RBI | BB | SO | LOB | AVG |
|---|---|---|---|---|---|---|---|---|
| Jeter, SS | 4 | 1 | 1 | 0 | 1 | 2 | 1 | .280 |
| Damon, LF | 5 | 0 | 1 | 0 | 0 | 0 | 3 | .269 |
| Teixeira, 1B | 5 | 1 | 2 | 3 | 0 | 1 | 2 | .174 |
| Rodriguez, 3B | 3 | 1 | 1 | 0 | 2 | 1 | 3 | .368 |
|   Guzman, PR | 0 | 0 | 0 | 0 | 0 | 0 | 0 | .000 |
| Matsui, DH | 3 | 1 | 1 | 1 | 2 | 0 | 3 | .294 |
|   Gardner, PR | 0 | 0 | 0 | 0 | 0 | 0 | 0 | .667 |
| Cano, 2B | 4 | 0 | 1 | 2 | 0 | 1 | 3 | .238 |
| Swisher, RF | 5 | 0 | 0 | 0 | 0 | 1 | 4 | .118 |
| Cabrera, CF | 4 | 1 | 2 | 0 | 0 | 2 | 0 | .381 |
| Molina, C | 1 | 0 | 0 | 0 | 0 | 0 | 0 | .333 |
|   Posada, PH-C | 2 | 1 | 0 | 0 | 1 | 1 | 1 | .267 |
| TOTALS | 36 | 6 | 9 | 6 | 6 | 9 | 20 | |

BATTING:

2B: Teixeira (1, Oliver); Rodriguez (2, Lackey); Cabrera (2, Lackey). 3B: Cano (2, Jepsen).
TB: Jeter; Damon; Teixeira 3; Rodriguez 2; Matsui; Cano 3; Cabrera 3. RBI: Teixeira 3 (3);
Matsui (3); Cano 2 (4). 2-out RBI: Teixeira 3, Matsui; Cano 2. Runners left in scoring posi-
tion, 2 out: Matsui; Cano 2; Swisher 3. Team LOB: 10.

FIELDING:

DP: 2 (Cano-Jeter-Teixeira, Rodriguez-Cano-Teixeira)

*Cabrera*

Aybar to third on a groundout to first base.

With two outs, a runner at third base and a 6-5 lead, Phil Hughes replaced Marte on the mound.

Hughes walked Torii Hunter before giving up back-to-back singles to Vladimir Guerrero and first baseman Kendry Morales, giving the Angels a 7-6 lead.

The Yankees went down in order in the eighth against Jered Weaver, but nearly tied the game in the final frame.

With two outs in the ninth, Angels closer Brian Fuentes intentionally walked Rodriguez, walked Matsui and hit Cano with a pitch to load the bases.

Nick Swisher got Fuentes to a full-count before popping up a fastball for the final out of the game.

| LOS ANGELES | AB | R | H | RBI | BB | SO | LOB | AVG |
|---|---|---|---|---|---|---|---|---|
| Figgins, 3B | 3 | 1 | 0 | 0 | 1 | 1 | 2 | .105 |
| Abreu, RF | 5 | 1 | 1 | 1 | 0 | 1 | 3 | .143 |
| Hunter, CF | 2 | 2 | 2 | 2 | 2 | 0 | 0 | .316 |
| Guerrero, DH | 4 | 1 | 2 | 2 | 0 | 0 | 2 | .304 |
| Morales, 1B | 4 | 0 | 2 | 2 | 0 | 1 | 1 | .200 |
| Izturis, 2B | 4 | 0 | 0 | 0 | 0 | 1 | 3 | .111 |
| Rivera, LF | 4 | 0 | 1 | 0 | 0 | 0 | 1 | .143 |
| Willits, PR-LF | 0 | 0 | 0 | 0 | 0 | 0 | 0 | .000 |
| Mathis, C | 4 | 1 | 3 | 0 | 0 | 1 | 1 | .600 |
| Aybar, SS | 3 | 1 | 1 | 0 | 1 | 0 | 2 | .294 |
| TOTALS | 33 | 7 | 12 | 7 | 4 | 5 | 15 | |

**BATTING:**

2B: Abreu (2, Burnett); Guerrero (2, Burnett); Rivera (1, Chamberlain); Mathis (4, Burnett). TB: Abreu 2; Hunter 2; Guerrero 3; Morales 2; Rivera 2; Mathis 4; Aybar 2. RBI: Abreu (1); Hunter 2 (2); Guerrero 2 (4); Morales 2 (4). 2-out RBI: Guerrero; Morales. Runners left in scoring position, 2 out: Abreu 2; Morales; Izturis; Aybar. S: Figgins. GIDP: Rivera; Aybar. Team LOB: 7.

**BASERUNNING:**

SB: Hunter (1, 2nd base off Burnett/Molina); Aybar (3, 2nd base off Rivera/Posada).

| N.Y. YANKEES | IP | H | R | ER | BB | SO | HR | ERA |
|---|---|---|---|---|---|---|---|---|
| Burnett | 6 | 8 | 6 | 6 | 3 | 3 | 0 | 5.84 |
| Marte (H, 1) | ⅔ | 0 | 0 | 0 | 0 | 0 | 0 | 0.00 |
| Hughes (BS, 1) (L, 0-1) | ⅓ | 2 | 1 | 1 | 1 | 1 | 0 | 3.38 |
| Chamberlain | ⅓ | 2 | 0 | 0 | 0 | 1 | 0 | 9.00 |
| Rivera | ⅔ | 0 | 0 | 0 | 0 | 0 | 0 | 0.00 |

| LOS ANGELES | IP | H | R | ER | BB | SO | HR | ERA |
|---|---|---|---|---|---|---|---|---|
| Lackey | 6⅔ | 6 | 3 | 3 | 3 | 7 | 0 | 3.65 |
| Oliver (BS, 1) | 0 | 2 | 3 | 3 | 1 | 0 | 0 | 7.36 |
| Jepsen (W, 1-0) | ⅓ | 1 | 0 | 0 | 0 | 0 | 0 | 2.45 |
| Weaver (H, 1) | 1 | 0 | 0 | 0 | 0 | 2 | 0 | 4.50 |
| Fuentes (S, 1) | 1 | 0 | 0 | 0 | 2 | 0 | 0 | 3.00 |

Burnett pitched to two batters in the 7th.

WP: Burnett.

IBB: Rodriguez (by Oliver), Rodriguez (by Fuentes).

HBP: Cano (by Fuentes).

Pitches-strikes: Burnett 89-55; Marte 4-3; Hughes 18-9; Chamberlain 10-8; Rivera 7-5. Lackey 104-62; Oliver 8-3; Jepsen 5-3; Weaver 11-8; Fuentes 24-10.

Ground outs-fly outs: Burnett 10-5; Marte 2-0; Hughes 0-0; Chamberlain 0-0; Rivera 0-2. Lackey 7-6; Oliver 0-0; Jepsen 0-1; Weaver 1-0; Fuentes 0-3.

Batters faced: Burnett 27; Marte 2; Hughes 4; Chamberlain 3; Rivera 2. Lackey 29; Oliver 3; Jepsen 2; Weaver 3; Fuentes 6.

Inherited runners-scored: Marte 2-1; Hughes 1-1; Rivera 2-0. Oliver 3-3; Jepsen 2-2.

Umpires: HP: Fieldin Culbreth. 1B: Dale Scott. 2B: Tim McClelland. 3B: Laz Diaz. LF: Bill Miller. RF: Jerry Layne.

Weather: 78 degrees, sunny. Wind: 8 mph. T: 3:34. Att: 45,113.

# PRIDE OF OCTOBER

BY NATHAN MACIBORSKI

## YANKS VETERANS HELP DELIVER FIRST PENNANT SINCE 2003

### ANGELS ② YANKEES ⑤

I t was déjà vu all over again. Andy Pettitte pitched brilliantly, Derek Jeter drew a key walk, and in the end, Mariano Rivera and Jorge Posada embraced after an emotional victory.

It could have been one of those Yankees classics they show on the YES Network during rain delays. But this was 2009, and a 5-2 victory over the Angels in front of an electric Yankee Stadium crowd meant that the Yankees were headed to their 40th Fall Classic.

"I'm extremely happy for the guys in that [club-house], for the Boss, his children, all the people that put all this hard work in to put this team together," said Yankees manager Joe Girardi after the American League Championship Series Game 6 win. "Brian Cashman has done a great job. Our developmental people have done a great job. You think about all the people that

have come up and played and had an impact on our season so far — all the young kids — it's just been a real team effort."

"This is what you play for, a chance to get back to the World Series," Jeter said. "I'm real proud of this team, but we still have four more wins to get."

Pettitte tossed 6¹/₃ innings of one-run ball to clinch a series for the second time in 2009. Making his 38th postseason start, the 37-year-old lefthander moved to the top of the all-time list with his 16th postseason win, 10 of which were saved by Rivera. Pettitte's fifth career series-clinching victory also established a new record.

With the Yankees trailing, 1-0, in the bottom of the fourth, Jeter worked an eight-pitch walk to load the bases for Johnny Damon, who deliv-

*Pettitte*

*Rivera*

ered a two-run single to center. Two batters later, Alex Rodriguez drew a bases-loaded walk that sent Angels starter Joe Saunders to the showers.

Another déjà vu moment came in the sixth inning, when Pettitte faced Vladimir Guerrero with two outs, a runner on first and a 3-1 lead. In the exact same situation in Game 3, Guerrero blasted a two-run homer, but this time, Pettitte emerged relatively unscathed. Guerrero golfed an 0-2 pitch down the right-field line for a double that Torii Hunter failed to score on.

After Juan Rivera drove Pettitte's 99th pitch to right field for a one-out single in the seventh, Girardi removed his former battery mate from the game. With flashbulbs popping and a roaring crowd on its feet, Pettitte doffed his cap as he headed into the dugout, then watched Joba Chamberlain induce two straight ground balls to end the inning.

"There's a lot of guys that can do a lot of things down there [in the bullpen]," Chamberlain said. "I was just blessed to be able to come in after Andy and give the ball to Mo. I'm still kind of slapping myself in the face."

Girardi called upon Rivera to begin the eighth, and the closer allowed his first post-season earned run at home since 2000. But thanks to two Angels errors, the Yankees tacked on two insurance runs in the bottom half of the inning. In the ninth, Rivera retired the side in order for his 37th postseason save and his seventh trip to the World Series.

"It feels like a lot longer than six years," Rivera said. "We fought hard for this one."

"It is really not a surprise that we are here," CC Sabathia said. "I hate to sound like that, but this is a really good team. We get along, [and] we have fun. This is what you get."

THE YANKEES TACKED ON TWO INSURANCE RUNS IN THE BOTTOM OF THE 8TH THANKS TO TWO ANGELS ERRORS.

# RODRIGUEZ ON A ROLL

**S**ometimes being the first player on the field for warm-ups is indicative of a player's need for extra practice. This was far from the case for Alex Rodriguez.

Nearly 30 minutes before his teammates took the field for Game 6 batting practice, Rodriguez — who through the first five games of the American League Championship Series hit .368 — was already having a catch on the infield grass. He was just that locked in and ready to go.

Rodriguez capped his standout ALCS by going 2-for-2 with three walks in the clincher. He reached base safely in his final eight plate appearances of the series. For the series, Rodriguez hit .429 (9-for-21) with three home runs, six RBI and eight walks.

"For me, with no expectations and trusting my teammates and taking the walks and doing the little things, you end up doing big things," Rodriguez said. "That's the lesson for me."

— Craig Tapper

*Johnny Damon*

**ALDS** 2009    GAME **6**

LOS ANGELES ANGELS OF ANAHEIM    2
NEW YORK YANKEES    5

| | 1 2 3 4 5 6 7 8 9 | R | H | E |
|---|---|---|---|---|
| ANGELS | 0 0 1 0 0 0 0 1 0 | 2 | 9 | 2 |
| YANKEES | 0 0 0 3 0 0 0 2 X | 5 | 9 | 0 |

| LOS ANGELES | AB | R | H | RBI | BB | SO | LOB | AVG |
|---|---|---|---|---|---|---|---|---|
| Figgins, 3B | 4 | 1 | 1 | 0 | 0 | 0 | 1 | .130 |
| Abreu, RF | 4 | 0 | 1 | 1 | 0 | 1 | 1 | .160 |
| Hunter, CF | 4 | 0 | 1 | 0 | 0 | 1 | 2 | .304 |
| Guerrero, DH | 4 | 0 | 3 | 1 | 0 | 1 | 0 | .370 |
| Willits, PR-DH | 0 | 0 | 0 | 0 | 0 | 0 | 0 | .000 |
| Morales, 1B | 4 | 0 | 0 | 0 | 0 | 0 | 4 | .167 |
| Kendrick, 2B | 3 | 0 | 0 | 0 | 1 | 1 | 0 | .286 |
| Rivera, LF | 4 | 0 | 2 | 0 | 0 | 0 | 1 | .200 |
| Mathis, C | 2 | 1 | 1 | 0 | 0 | 1 | 1 | .583 |
| Izturis, PH | 1 | 0 | 0 | 0 | 0 | 0 | 1 | .100 |
| Napoli, C | 0 | 0 | 0 | 0 | 0 | 0 | 0 | .111 |
| Matthews, PH | 1 | 0 | 0 | 0 | 0 | 1 | 0 | .000 |
| Aybar, SS | 3 | 0 | 0 | 0 | 0 | 1 | 3 | .250 |
| TOTALS | 34 | 2 | 9 | 2 | 1 | 7 | 14 | |

**BATTING:**

2B: Guerrero (3, Pettitte); Mathis (5, Pettitte). TB: Figgins; Abreu; Hunter; Guerrero 4; Rivera 2; Mathis 2. RBI: Abreu (2), Guerrero (5). 2-out RBI: Abreu; Guerrero. Runners left in scoring position, 2 out: Morales 2. GIDP: Aybar. Team LOB: 6.

**FIELDING:**

E: Kendrick (1, missed catch); Kazmir (1, throw). DP: 3 (Kendrick-Aybar-Morales; Figgins-Morales; Morales-Aybar-Morales).

| N.Y. YANKEES | AB | R | H | RBI | BB | SO | LOB | AVG |
|---|---|---|---|---|---|---|---|---|
| Jeter, SS | 2 | 1 | 0 | 0 | 3 | 0 | 2 | .259 |
| Damon, LF | 4 | 0 | 2 | 2 | 1 | 0 | 3 | .300 |
| Teixeira, 1B | 4 | 0 | 2 | 1 | 0 | 0 | 2 | .222 |
| Rodriguez, 3B | 2 | 0 | 2 | 1 | 3 | 0 | 0 | .429 |
| Posada, C | 5 | 0 | 0 | 0 | 0 | 1 | 10 | .200 |
| Matsui, DH | 4 | 0 | 0 | 0 | 0 | 0 | 1 | .238 |
| Cano, 2B | 2 | 2 | 1 | 0 | 2 | 1 | 0 | .261 |
| Swisher, RF | 3 | 1 | 1 | 0 | 0 | 1 | 1 | .150 |
| Gardner, PR-CF | 0 | 1 | 0 | 0 | 0 | 0 | 0 | .667 |
| Cabrera, CF-RF | 2 | 0 | 1 | 0 | 0 | 0 | 0 | .391 |
| TOTALS | 28 | 5 | 9 | 4 | 9 | 3 | 19 | |

**BATTING:**

TB: Damon 2; Teixeira 2; Rodriguez 2; Cano; Swisher; Cabrera. RBI: Damon 2 (5); Teixeira (4); Rodriguez (6). Runners left in scoring position, 2 out: Damon 2; Posada 3. S: Swisher; Cabrera 2. SF: Teixeira. GIDP: Teixeira; Posada 2. Team LOB: 12.

**FIELDING:**

Outfield assists: Swisher (Guerrero at 1st base). DP: 2 (Cano-Teixeira; Swisher-Teixeira).

| LOS ANGELES | IP | H | R | ER | BB | SO | HR | ERA |
|---|---|---|---|---|---|---|---|---|
| Saunders (L, 0-1) | 3⅓ | 7 | 3 | 3 | 5 | 0 | 0 | 4.35 |
| Oliver | 2⅔ | 1 | 0 | 0 | 1 | 2 | 0 | 4.26 |
| Santana | 1 | 1 | 1 | 0 | 1 | 0 | 0 | 1.59 |
| Kazmir | ⅔ | 0 | 1 | 0 | 1 | 0 | 0 | 7.71 |
| Weaver | ⅓ | 0 | 0 | 0 | 1 | 1 | 0 | 4.26 |

| N.Y. YANKEES | IP | H | R | ER | BB | SO | HR | ERA |
|---|---|---|---|---|---|---|---|---|
| Pettitte (W, 1-0) | 6⅓ | 7 | 1 | 1 | 1 | 6 | 0 | 2.84 |
| Chamberlain (H, 1) | ⅔ | 0 | 0 | 0 | 0 | 0 | 0 | 5.40 |
| Rivera (S, 2) | 2 | 2 | 1 | 1 | 0 | 1 | 0 | 1.29 |

Santana pitched to one batter in the 8th.

Pitches-strikes: Saunders 83-42; Oliver 33-20; Santana 16-8; Kazmir 22-12; Weaver 10-4. Pettitte 99-64; Chamberlain 7-4; Rivera 34-23.

Ground outs-fly outs: Saunders 7-3; Oliver 5-1; Santana 2-1; Kazmir 1-1; Weaver 0-0. Pettitte 8-4; Chamberlain 2-0; Rivera 4-1.

Batters Faced: Saunders 22; Oliver 8; Santana 4; Kazmir 5; Weaver 2. Pettitte 25; Chamberlain 2; Rivera 8.

Inherited runners-scored: Oliver 3-0; Kazmir 1-1; Weaver 2-0. Chamberlain 1-0.

Umpires: HP: Dale Scott. 1B: Tim McClelland. 2B: Laz Diaz. 3B: Bill Miller. LF: Jerry Layne. RF: Fieldin Culbreth.

Weather: 58 degrees, partly cloudy. Wind: 8 mph. T: 3:40 Att: 50,173.

# ALEX RODRIGUEZ

BY MARK FEINSAND

Before the postseason began, Alex Rodriguez had a calm about him that hadn't been present in any October he had experienced during his six years in pinstripes.

"Right now, I'm playing with the house's money, basically," Rodriguez said. "I feel like I have nothing to lose."

Having endured an unusual Spring Training that included a potentially career-altering hip surgery, A-Rod was unsure that he would be able to contribute to the Yankees' 2009 campaign at all. But after rejoining the lineup with a bang — he blasted the first pitch he saw in his May 8 return for a three-run home run — Rodriguez put together an impressive season that saw him hit 30 home runs while driving in 100 RBI, reaching the two milestones with an unlikely two-homer, seven-RBI performance in the final inning of his season.

That dramatic finish set the stage for one of the most remarkable turnarounds in postseason history, one that helped Rodriguez exorcise his playoff demons once and for all.

A-Rod's postseason began in familiar fashion with him coming up short in his first two American League Division Series at-bats — both with runners on base. But as he came to bat in the fifth, Rodriguez singled in Derek Jeter to help the Yankees build a lead against the Twins, one he lengthened two innings later with another run-scoring hit.

"I'm sure it makes him feel good inside," said manager Joe Girardi. "Whenever you contribute, it's important. It puts you in a good place."

Rodriguez was clearly in that good place and had no plans of vacating it. He went on to torch the Twins for a .455 average, two home runs — both late-inning, game-tying blasts — and six RBI in the Yankees' three-game sweep of Minnesota.

The surge continued in the American League Championship Series against the Angels. Rodriguez hit .429 with three home runs and six RBI in the Yankees' six-game series win, thrusting A-Rod into his first career World Series. But Rodriguez wasn't satisfied. Not yet.

"In order to win a World Series, you have to get there," A-Rod said. "We've done that. Now we need four more wins."

An 0-for-8, six-strikeout start to the Fall Classic had many people speculating that Rodriguez was back to his old ways, gripping the bat too tightly each time he stepped to the plate. But after Cole Hamels drilled Rodriguez with a pitch in his first plate appearance in Game 3, the third baseman snapped out of his funk, belting a home run in his next trip to the plate. The next night, Rodriguez delivered a go-ahead RBI double in the top of the ninth, helping the Yankees seize a 3-games-to-1 lead in the World Series.

"There's no question; I've never had a bigger hit," Rodriguez said.

Rodriguez wound up hitting .417 with a home run and six RBI in the final four games of the series, helping the Yankees to their first World Series title since 2000 and filling a gaping hole on his legendary résumé.

"Alex deserves this," Mark Teixeira said. "He's one of the greatest players of all time. He went through a lot this year, and now he's a world champion."

# 09
## WORLD SERIES

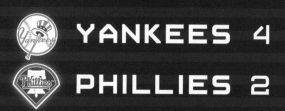

YANKEES 4

PHILLIES 2

# THE BIG

# 3

**SABATHIA**

**BURNETT**

**PETTITTE**

BY BOB KLAPISCH

THEY SAID IT COULDN'T BE DONE — AND IF TRIED,
BEWARE OF THE CONSEQUENCES — BECAUSE NO
MODERN-DAY BASEBALL TEAM WOULD DARE GO INTO
THE POSTSEASON WITH A THREE-MAN ROTATION.

Crazy? It was masochism if you adhered to the new millennium philosophy, which says it takes four starters, not three, to win a championship. But try telling that to manager Joe Girardi, whose Yankees flattened everyone in their postseason path with only CC Sabathia, A.J. Burnett and Andy Pettitte toeing the rubber to start the games.

It wasn't a perfect equation, and it certainly wasn't easy. But by the time it was over, as the Yankees turned Yankee Stadium into an open-air asylum after Game 6 of the World Series, they became the first team in 18 years to sail through the post-

enough to almost call it quits after 2008.

The Yankees took a chance on Pettitte, signing him to a one-year deal that turned out to be one of the season's best bargains. Pettitte won all three clinching games during the Yankees' run, breathlessly telling reporters at the conclusion of the World Series, "This is what I came back for."

The sense of history wasn't lost on any of the Yankees. The franchise's last winning three-man rotation dated back to 1962, when Whitey Ford, Ralph Terry and Bill Stafford combined to take down the San Francisco Giants. But even that threesome needed help from multiple rainouts to get

the postseason for the first time since 2003.

After struggling in Game 3, Pettitte admitted before Game 6 that he had no idea how his arm would respond. Girardi, however, had a premonition. The fact that Pettitte was making his final start of the season would actually help him because a pitcher can spend whatever is left in the tank without worrying about the ramifications.

The Yankees knew they were gambling on a 37-year-old arm, but the dividend was huge. When Pettitte walked off the mound in the sixth inning en route to his 18th career postseason victory, the Stadium crowd didn't just cheer. They rose as one

season without a four-man rotation.

Taking their cue from the 1991 Twins' Jack Morris, Scott Erickson and Kevin Tapani, the Yankees' trio pitched on short rest in both the American League Championship Series and World Series, building to a crescendo when Pettitte outperformed Pedro Martinez — who was working on full rest — in the finale in New York.

It was an especially poignant moment for Pettitte, who had struggled with elbow injuries in recent years and, after nearly 3,000 career regular-season innings, was weary

through a seven-game series.

The 2009 Yankees were afforded no such shortcuts. In the ALCS, Sabathia worked on three days' rest in Game 4 — although Burnett and Pettitte closed out the series on normal rest because of a scheduled off-day between Games 4 and 5.

But the war with the Phillies was just that — a war. Only three days separated Sabathia's starts in Games 1 and 4, and Burnett was similarly taxed in Game 5. The real drama belonged to Pettitte, though, who was asked to work on short rest in

in what could only be described as a public love-in.

The response needed no translation: It was New York's way of saying thank you to Pettitte and the Big Three.

# CLIFF HANGER

BY KRISTINA M. DODGE

## LEE OUT-DUELS FRIEND AND FORMER TEAMMATE SABATHIA IN FALL CLASSIC OPENER

PHILLIES  YANKEES

**Y**ankees postseason stalwart CC Sabathia was good. Unfortunately for the Bombers, Phillies starter Cliff Lee was better, pitching a complete game on his way to leading his club to a 6-1 victory in Game 1 of the World Series at Yankee Stadium.

"[Lee] was great tonight," said Yankees manager Joe Girardi. "He kept us off balance. He got us to chase some pitches when we were down in the count, up in the zone. He used his

cutter very well, [and] he used his curveball really well."

If the matchup looked familiar, that's because it was. The former Cleveland Indians teammates and back-to-back American League Cy Young Award winners faced off in the Yankees' home opener on April 16 with similar end results. The Indians beat the Bombers, 10-2, behind a one-run, six-inning performance by Lee. This time, the lefty — in new threads — went the

SABATHIA'S ONLY COSTLY MISTAKES OF THE NIGHT CAME IN THE THIRD AND SIXTH INNINGS, WHEN UTLEY TAGGED HIM FOR TWO SOLO HOME RUNS, BOTH WITH TWO STRIKES. UTLEY BECAME THE FIRST LEFTHANDER TO HIT A LONGBALL OFF OF SABATHIA AT YANKEE STADIUM.

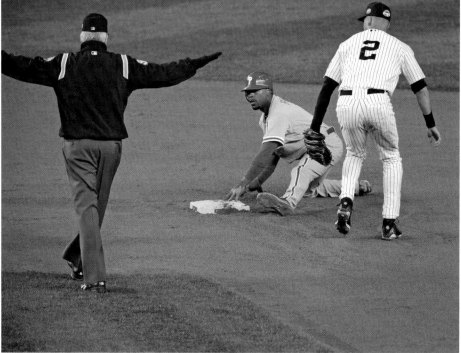

distance, striking out 10 and walking no one, to hand the Yankees their first home loss of the postseason.

"He's been their ace for a reason," said Derek Jeter, who laid claim to three of Lee's six hits allowed. "He knows what he's doing. I don't care what league he's pitching in. He's had a lot of success."

Sabathia started the game with two quick outs, retiring shortstop Jimmy Rollins and centerfielder Shane Victorino, but soon worked himself into a jam. The southpaw loaded the bases with a walk to second baseman Chase Utley, a double to first baseman Ryan Howard and a walk to right fielder Jayson Werth before getting Raul Ibanez to ground out.

He escaped the 24-pitch inning without allowing a run and settled in. His only costly mistakes of the night came in the third and sixth innings, when Utley tagged him for two

# AMERICA'S FINEST

**G**ame 1 of the 2009 World Series had special meaning before the first pitch was even thrown.

First lady Michelle Obama and second lady Jill Biden took part in a pregame ceremony to raise awareness for Welcome Back Veterans, a Major League Baseball and McCormick Foundation joint initiative.

The charitable program is designed to support returning Iraq and Afghanistan veterans and their families with mental health treatment and job opportunities. To date, Welcome Back Veterans has awarded $5.8 million in grants to not-for-profit agencies.

"I want to thank everyone in Major League Baseball for all that they did for our veterans," Obama said.

"This has been a phenomenal effort to bring exposure and awareness, and we are grateful that Major League Baseball has decided to take on this issue at a time that is so important."

Obama and Biden were escorted to the pitcher's mound by Yankees legend Yogi Berra, who served in World War II. After the trio arrived on the mound, Tony Odierno, who lost his arm during the war in Iraq, tossed out the game's ceremonial first pitch. Odierno, who received a Bronze Star for valor and a Purple Heart, is a member of the Yankees front office.

— Alfred Santasiere III

---

solo home runs, both with two strikes. Utley became the first lefthander to hit a longball off of Sabathia at Yankee Stadium, and the homers were the first and second the Yankees had given up at home during the postseason.

"He was pitching me tough," said Utley. "The approach I had was to lay off the slider because the slider is a tough one to hit on the barrel and to try to hit his fastball, and I was able to do that. He left one kind of in the middle of the plate, and you can't miss those pitches against that type of pitcher."

With the Yankees down, 2-0, Girardi turned the game over to the bullpen after the seventh, and the Yankees relief corps proceeded to allow four runs on five hits over the next two innings.

The Yankees' only run of the evening came in the ninth on a Rollins' throwing error. With men on first and second and no outs, Mark Teixeira hit one up the middle. Utley fielded, then tossed the ball to the Phillies shortstop, who stepped on second to get Johnny Damon out, but threw over the head of Howard at

first, allowing Jeter to score. Lee followed by striking out Alex Rodriguez and Jorge Posada to end the game.

Shortly after the final out, the Bombers had already refocused their energy.

"You move on — quick," said Rodriguez, who struck out three times. "You have to have a short memory. We need to win [Game 2], obviously. We need to go back to Philly, 1-1."

| PHILADELPHIA | AB | R | H | RBI | BB | SO | LOB | AVG |
|---|---|---|---|---|---|---|---|---|
| Rollins, SS | 4 | 2 | 1 | 0 | 1 | 0 | 0 | .250 |
| Victorino, CF | 4 | 1 | 1 | 1 | 1 | 0 | 0 | .250 |
| Utley, 2B | 4 | 2 | 2 | 2 | 1 | 1 | 4 | .500 |
| Howard, 1B | 5 | 0 | 2 | 1 | 0 | 2 | 2 | .400 |
| Werth, RF | 2 | 0 | 1 | 0 | 2 | 1 | 0 | .500 |
| Ibanez, DH | 4 | 0 | 1 | 2 | 0 | 2 | 4 | .250 |
| Francisco, LF | 3 | 0 | 0 | 0 | 1 | 0 | 2 | .000 |
| Feliz, 3B | 4 | 0 | 0 | 0 | 0 | 1 | 1 | .000 |
| Ruiz, C | 4 | 1 | 1 | 0 | 0 | 0 | 0 | .250 |
| TOTALS | 34 | 6 | 9 | 6 | 6 | 7 | 13 | |

**BATTING:**

2B: Howard 2 (2, Sabathia, Coke); Ruiz (1, Bruney). HR: Utley 2 (2, 3rd inning off Sabathia, 0 on, 2 out; 6th inning off Sabathia, 0 on, 1 out). TB: Rollins; Victorino; Utley 8; Howard 4; Werth; Ibanez; Ruiz 2. RBI: Victorino (1); Utley 2 (2); Howard (1); Ibanez 2 (2). 2-out RBI: Utley; Howard; Ibanez 2. Runners left in scoring position, 2 out: Ibanez 2; Francisco. GIDP: Feliz. Team LOB: 7.

**BASERUNNING:**

SB: Rollins (1, 2nd base off Hughes/Posada).

**FIELDING:**

E: Rollins (1, throw). DP: (Rollins-Howard).

**PHILADELPHIA PHILLIES**      6
**NEW YORK YANKEES**      1

| | 1 2 3 4 5 6 7 8 9 | R | H | E |
|---|---|---|---|---|
| PHILLIES | 0 0 1 0 0 1 0 2 2 | 6 | 9 | 1 |
| YANKEES | 0 0 0 0 0 0 0 0 1 | 1 | 6 | 0 |

| N.Y. YANKEES | AB | R | H | RBI | BB | SO | LOB | AVG |
|---|---|---|---|---|---|---|---|---|
| Jeter, SS | 4 | 1 | 3 | 0 | 0 | 1 | 0 | .750 |
| Damon, LF | 4 | 0 | 1 | 0 | 0 | 0 | 2 | .250 |
| Teixeira, 1B | 4 | 0 | 0 | 0 | 0 | 2 | 2 | .000 |
| Rodriguez, 3B | 4 | 0 | 0 | 0 | 0 | 3 | 1 | .000 |
| Posada, C | 4 | 0 | 1 | 0 | 0 | 2 | 1 | .250 |
| Matsui, DH | 3 | 0 | 1 | 0 | 0 | 1 | 1 | .333 |
| Cano, 2B | 3 | 0 | 0 | 0 | 0 | 0 | 2 | .000 |
| Swisher, RF | 3 | 0 | 0 | 0 | 0 | 1 | 0 | .000 |
| Cabrera, CF | 3 | 0 | 0 | 0 | 0 | 0 | 0 | .000 |
| TOTALS | 32 | 1 | 6 | 0 | 0 | 10 | 9 | |

**BATTING:**

2B: Jeter (1, Lee). TB: Jeter 4; Damon; Posada; Matsui. Runners left in scoring position, 2 out: Damon; Posada. Team LOB: 4

**FIELDING:**

Outfield assists: Swisher (Victorino at home). DP: (Rodriguez-Cano-Teixeira)

| PHILADELPHIA | IP | H | R | ER | BB | SO | HR | ERA |
|---|---|---|---|---|---|---|---|---|
| Lee (W, 1-0) | 9 | 6 | 1 | 0 | 0 | 10 | 0 | 0.00 |

| N.Y. YANKEES | IP | H | R | ER | BB | SO | HR | ERA |
|---|---|---|---|---|---|---|---|---|
| Sabathia (L, 0-1) | 7 | 4 | 2 | 2 | 3 | 6 | 2 | 2.57 |
| Hughes | 0 | 0 | 2 | 2 | 2 | 0 | 0 | — |
| Marte | ⅔ | 0 | 0 | 0 | 0 | 1 | 0 | 0.00 |
| Robertson | ⅓ | 1 | 0 | 0 | 1 | 0 | 0 | 0.00 |
| Bruney | ⅓ | 3 | 2 | 2 | 0 | 0 | 0 | 54.00 |
| Coke | ⅔ | 1 | 0 | 0 | 0 | 0 | 0 | 0.00 |

Hughes pitched to two batters in the 8th.

Pitches-strikes: Lee 122-80. Sabathia 113-70; Hughes 15-7; Marte 7-4; Robertson 13-6; Bruney 13-7; Coke 9-5.

Ground outs-fly outs: Lee 8-8. Sabathia 10-5; Hughes 0-0; Marte 0-1; Robertson 1-0; Bruney 0-1; Coke 0-1.

Batters faced: Lee 32. Sabathia 27; Hughes 2; Marte 2; Robertson 3; Bruney 4; Coke 2. Inherited runners-scored: Marte 2-0; Robertson 2-2; Coke 2-1.

Umpires: HP: Gerry Davis. 1B: Jeff Nelson. 2B: Brian Gorman. 3B: Mike Everitt. LF: Dana DeMuth. RF: Joe West.

Weather: 52 degrees, cloudy. Wind: 13 mph. T: 3:27. Att: 50,207.

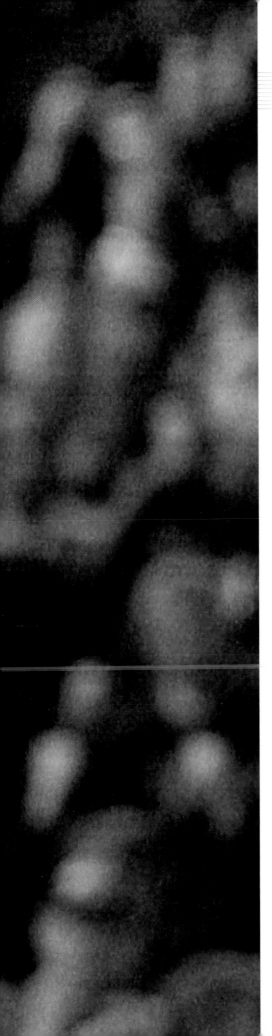

# BACK
## IN BUSINESS

BY CRAIG TAPPER

### BURNETT'S GEM HELPS EVEN FALL CLASSIC

## PHILLIES  1 YANKEES  3

**A.J.** Burnett hurled one of his best games in pinstripes, Mark Teixeira and Hideki Matsui chipped in solo homers, and the Yankees defeated the Phillies, 3-1, to knot the World Series at one game apiece.

"It's a terrible cliché, but it was a must-win," Teixeira said. "You don't want to go 0-2 into Philadelphia. If we went in there 0-2, it would have been a tough road for us."

One week earlier, Burnett had allowed four first-inning runs in Game 5 of the American League Championship Series, but the righty upped his game in his first Fall Classic appearance. He pitched seven innings and yielded one run on four hits while striking out nine Phillies.

Masterful from beginning to end, Burnett opened his start with a 1-2-3, 12-pitch first inning and closed the evening with a 1-2-3, 11-pitch seventh frame. He threw first-pitch strikes to the first 11 batters he faced.

"After last [night's Game 1], I just wanted to come out and set the tone early and be very aggressive," Burnett said. "My key was Strike 1 tonight I think. I threw a lot of first-pitch strikes and that allowed me to open up and expand the zone after that."

The Phillies took an early 1-0 lead when Matt Stairs grounded a two-out RBI single under the

LEADING OFF THE BOTTOM OF THE FOURTH
INNING, TEIXEIRA HIT A HOME RUN TO TIE
THE GAME AT 1-1. TWO INNINGS LATER,
MATSUI HIT A SOLO HOMER WITH TWO OUTS
TO GIVE THE YANKEES THEIR FIRST LEAD
OF THE SERIES.

glove of Alex Rodriguez in the second inning. Burnett escaped the inning without further trouble and kept the Phillies off the board in the third by striking out Ryan Howard with two outs and runners on first and second. Just two more runners reached base over Burnett's final four innings.

Phillies starter Pedro Martinez made his return to the Bronx. Yankees fans serenaded Martinez with chants of "Who's your daddy," in reference to a comment Martinez made in 2004 about his struggles against the Bombers, but Martinez was in complete control for most of his outing.

The Yankees offense, which failed to score an earned run against Phillies ace Cliff Lee in Game 1, was desperately seeking a spark, and it got the necessary ignition from a superb defensive play in the top of the fourth.

Following an 0-2 pitch with Raul Ibanez at bat and Jayson Werth on first, Jose Molina fired to Teixeira, who applied the tag on Werth as he attempted to make it back to the bag.

"I thought it was real important because it changed [Burnett's] pitch count," Yankees manager Joe Girardi said. "It got him through that inning. I thought it was extremely important."

Leading off the bottom of the inning, Teixeira hit a home run to tie the game at 1-1. Two innings later, Matsui hit a solo homer with two outs to give the Yankees their first lead of the Series.

The Yankees tacked on a run in the seventh on three consecutive singles by Jerry Hairston Jr., Melky Cabrera and Jorge Posada. With a two-run lead through seven frames, Girardi took no chances and called upon Mariano Rivera for a six-out save.

"Even in 1996, when I caught him and he was a set-up guy, he would go more than two innings at a time," Girardi said. "It's something he's accustomed to doing. It's not something we like to do during the season because we think it's important to keep him healthy for the long run, but it can be real effective for us."

And it was.

Though it took Mo 39 pitches — the most he had ever thrown in a World Series — he managed to hold the Phillies scoreless. In the eighth and ninth innings, the Phillies put a man in scoring position, but Rivera avoided further trouble by inducing a Chase Utley double play in the eighth and a Stairs strikeout to end the game.

# SPECIAL RECOGNITION

In 1996, 22-year-old Derek Jeter set the tone for his career not just by batting .314 and winning the American League Rookie of the Year Award, but also by establishing the Turn 2 Foundation.

Thirteen years later, Jeter was named the 2009 recipient of the Roberto Clemente Award, given annually to the Major League Baseball player who combines dedication to the community with outstanding skills on the field.

"[Jeter] is a man of great character and a strong sense of giving back," said MLB commissioner Bud Selig. "He has made a great impact on the young people of western Michigan, Tampa, Florida, and New York City, keeping them off drugs and alcohol and teaching them the values that will lead to a better and more fulfilling life."

The Turn 2 Foundation has awarded more than $10 million in grants for programs promoting healthy lifestyles.

Jeter joined Ron Guidry (1984) and Don Baylor (1985) as the only Yankees to win the award, which has been presented every year since 1971. In 1973, the award was named in honor of the Pirates' Hall of Fame right fielder, who was killed in a plane crash while aiding earthquake-ravaged Nicaragua.

— Nathan Maciborski

---

| PHILADELPHIA | AB | R | H | RBI | BB | SO | LOB | AVG |
|---|---|---|---|---|---|---|---|---|
| Rollins, SS | 2 | 0 | 0 | 0 | 2 | 1 | 1 | .167 |
| Victorino, CF | 4 | 0 | 1 | 0 | 0 | 1 | 2 | .250 |
| Utley, 2B | 3 | 0 | 0 | 0 | 1 | 0 | 2 | .286 |
| Howard, 1B | 4 | 0 | 0 | 0 | 0 | 4 | 2 | .222 |
| Werth, RF | 4 | 0 | 1 | 0 | 0 | 0 | 0 | .333 |
| Ibanez, LF | 4 | 1 | 2 | 0 | 0 | 2 | 0 | .375 |
| Stairs, DH | 4 | 0 | 1 | 1 | 0 | 2 | 1 | .250 |
| Feliz, 3B | 3 | 0 | 0 | 0 | 0 | 1 | 1 | .000 |
| Ruiz, C | 3 | 0 | 1 | 0 | 0 | 0 | 0 | .286 |
| TOTALS | 31 | 1 | 6 | 1 | 3 | 11 | 9 | |

**BATTING:**
2B: Ibanez 2 (2, Burnett, Rivera); Ruiz (2, Burnett). TB: Victorino; Werth; Ibanez 4; Stairs; Ruiz 2. RBI: Stairs (1). 2-out RBI: Stairs. Runners left in scoring position, 2 out: Victorino; Howard; Stairs. GIDP: Utley. Team LOB: 6.

**BASERUNNING:**
PO: Werth (1st base by Molina).

**FIELDING:**
DP: (Howard-Rollins).

| PHILADELPHIA PHILLIES | 1 |
|---|---|
| NEW YORK YANKEES | 3 |

| | 1 2 3 4 5 6 7 8 9 | R | H | E |
|---|---|---|---|---|
| PHILLIES | 0 1 0 0 0 0 0 0 0 | 1 | 6 | 0 |
| YANKEES | 0 0 0 1 0 1 1 0 X | 3 | 8 | 0 |

*Jay-Z and Alicia Keys*

| N.Y. YANKEES | AB | R | H | RBI | BB | SO | LOB | AVG |
|---|---|---|---|---|---|---|---|---|
| Jeter, SS | 4 | 0 | 1 | 0 | 0 | 3 | 3 | .500 |
| Damon, LF | 4 | 0 | 0 | 0 | 0 | 1 | 4 | .125 |
| Teixeira, 1B | 3 | 1 | 1 | 1 | 0 | 1 | 0 | .143 |
| Rodriguez, 3B | 4 | 0 | 0 | 0 | 0 | 3 | 1 | .000 |
| Matsui, DH | 3 | 1 | 2 | 1 | 1 | 1 | 1 | .500 |
| Cano, 2B | 4 | 0 | 1 | 0 | 0 | 0 | 2 | .143 |
| Hairston, RF | 3 | 0 | 1 | 0 | 0 | 1 | 2 | .333 |
| Gardner, PR-CF | 1 | 1 | 0 | 0 | 0 | 1 | 2 | .000 |
| Cabrera, CF-RF | 3 | 0 | 1 | 0 | 0 | 1 | 0 | .167 |
| Molina, C | 1 | 0 | 0 | 0 | 1 | 0 | 0 | .000 |
| Posada, PH-C | 1 | 0 | 1 | 1 | 0 | 0 | 0 | .400 |
| TOTALS | 31 | 3 | 8 | 3 | 2 | 12 | 15 | |

**BATTING:**
2B: Jeter (2, Martinez). HR: Teixeira (1, 4th inning off Martinez, 0 on, 0 out); Matsui (1, 6th inning off Martinez, 0 on, 2 out). TB: Jeter 2; Teixeira 4; Matsui 5; Cano; Hairston; Cabrera; Posada. RBI: Teixeira (1); Matsui (1); Posada (1). 2-out RBI: Matsui. Runners left in scoring position, 2 out: Damon; Gardner. Team LOB: 7.

**FIELDING:**
DP: (Cano-Jeter-Teixeira). PO: Molina (Werth at 1st base).

| PHILADELPHIA | IP | H | R | ER | BB | SO | HR | ERA |
|---|---|---|---|---|---|---|---|---|
| Martinez (L, 0-1) | 6 | 6 | 3 | 3 | 2 | 8 | 2 | 4.50 |
| Park | ⅓ | 1 | 0 | 0 | 0 | 1 | 0 | 0.00 |
| Eyre | ⅔ | 0 | 0 | 0 | 0 | 0 | 0 | 0.00 |
| Madson | 1 | 1 | 0 | 0 | 0 | 3 | 0 | 0.00 |

| N.Y. YANKEES | IP | H | R | ER | BB | SO | HR | ERA |
|---|---|---|---|---|---|---|---|---|
| Burnett (W, 1-0) | 7 | 4 | 1 | 1 | 2 | 9 | 0 | 1.29 |
| Rivera (S, 1) | 2 | 2 | 0 | 0 | 1 | 2 | 0 | 0.00 |

Martinez pitched to two batters in the 7th.

IBB: Utley (by Burnett). HBP: Teixeira (by Madson).

Pitches-strikes: Martinez 107-72; Park 7-6; Eyre 2-2; Madson 18-13. Burnett 108-68; Rivera 39-26.

Ground outs-fly outs: Martinez 1-9; Park 0-0; Eyre 0-1; Madson 0-0. Burnett 5-6; Rivera 3-1.

Batters faced: Martinez 26; Park 2; Eyre 1; Madson 5. Burnett 26; Rivera 8.
Inherited runners-scored: Park 2-1; Eyre 2-0.

Umpires: HP: Jeff Nelson. 1B: Brian Gorman. 2B: Mike Everitt. 3B: Dana DeMuth. LF: Joe West. RF: Gerry Davis.

Weather: 52 degrees, cloudy. Wind: 9 mph. T: 3:25. Att: 50,181.

# STRONG ARM, STRONG BAT

BY ALFRED SANTASIERE III

## PETTITTE'S SIX-INNING PERFORMANCE ON THE MOUND AND RBI SINGLE HELP YANKS TAKE SERIES LEAD

YANKEES  8 PHILLIES  5

**A**ndy Pettitte battled the Phillies on the mound and surprised them at the plate during the Yankees' 8-5 victory in Game 3 of the World Series.

With the Yankees trailing, 3-2, in the top of the fifth inning, the southpaw silenced the Citizens Bank Park crowd by sending a bloop single off Phillies starter Cole Hamels into centerfield. The clutch hit scored Nick Swisher to tie the game.

"I've got a few World Series hits, and now I've got an RBI," Pettitte said. "I'm pretty happy about that."

Behind Pettitte's six-inning performance in which he gave up four runs, the Yankees took a 2-games-to-1 lead in the Fall Classic.

Philadelphia opened the scoring in the second inning, when Jayson Werth drove a 3-2 offering into the left-field seats.

After Pettitte struck out Raul Ibanez for the first out, the lefthander gave up a double to Pedro Feliz, walked Carlos Ruiz and surrendered a bunt single to Hamels. With the bases loaded and one out, Jimmy Rollins worked a five-pitch walk that advanced the runners and gave the Phillies a 2-0 lead.

Before Pettitte could get out of the second, Shane Victorino hit a sacrifice fly to left field, scoring the Phillies' third run.

Two innings later, the Yankees narrowed the Phillies' lead to 3-2.

With Mark Teixeira on first base and one out, Alex Rodriguez drilled a pitch just to the left of the right-field foul pole, where it bounced off the lens of a television camera and back onto the field. The hit was originally ruled a double, but after a review, the umpires changed their call to a home run.

"That was a big hit for us because it really got us going," said manager Joe Girardi. "Alex has been so good for us in the playoffs. He's a big reason we are at this point."

After Pettitte's RBI single in the fifth, Derek Jeter moved the pitcher to second base with a single to centerfield. Johnny Damon cleared the bases with a double, giving the Yankees a 5-3 advantage.

After Hamels walked Teixeira, Philadelphia skipper Charlie Manuel pulled the Phillies starter. In $4^{1}/_{3}$ innings of work, Hamels gave up five earned runs.

The Yankees lit up the scoreboard again in the sixth, when Swisher hit a solo home run off J.A. Happ, expanding the Yankees' lead to 6-3.

The longball was especially important for Swisher, who came into the game with a .114 World Series average and was not in the lineup

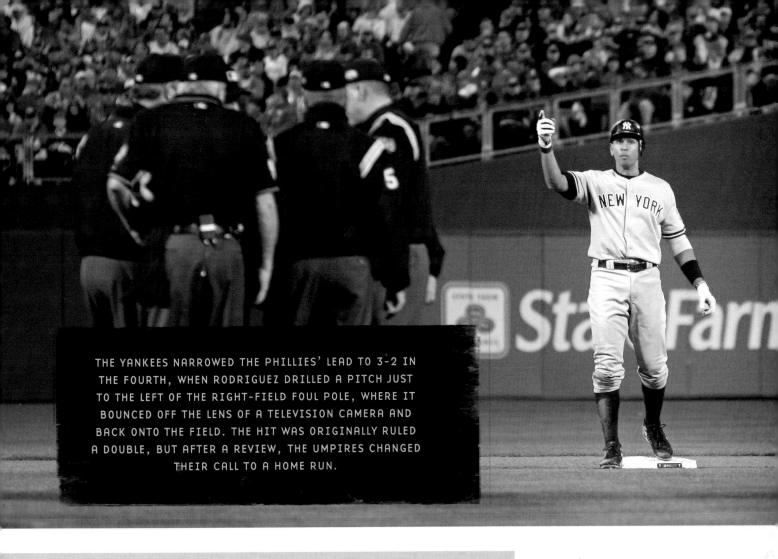

THE YANKEES NARROWED THE PHILLIES' LEAD TO 3-2 IN THE FOURTH, WHEN RODRIGUEZ DRILLED A PITCH JUST TO THE LEFT OF THE RIGHT-FIELD FOUL POLE, WHERE IT BOUNCED OFF THE LENS OF A TELEVISION CAMERA AND BACK ONTO THE FIELD. THE HIT WAS ORIGINALLY RULED A DOUBLE, BUT AFTER A REVIEW, THE UMPIRES CHANGED THEIR CALL TO A HOME RUN.

# PLAY IT AGAIN, ALEX

Trailing, 3-0, in the fourth inning, the Yankees were in need of a spark. They got one off the bat of Alex Rodriguez thanks to the first ever use of instant replay in post-season history.

With a runner on first and one out, Rodriguez swatted an 0-1 pitch from Cole Hamels down the right-field line. The ball seemed to strike the top of the wall and bounce back on the field for a double, but after video review, the umpiring crew determined that Rodriguez had hit a homer. The ball had actually struck a television camera that was above the wall.

"I wasn't 100 percent sure, but our coaches started yelling they thought it hit the camera," said Yankees manager Joe Girardi. "My eyes aren't great, so it was hard for me to see."

The use of instant replay was instituted during the 2008 season, and Rodriguez also hit the first-ever regular-season reviewed homer.

— Craig Tapper

for Game 2.

"One hit turns things around," Swisher said. "My teammates and the coaching staff really helped me through this tough time."

Werth led off the bottom of the sixth with his second solo homer of the game, which narrowed the Yankees' lead to two runs.

The Yankees scored their seventh run of the game in the seventh inning, when Jorge Posada collected a two-out single, plating Damon.

An inning later, pinch-hitter Hideki Matsui made it an 8-4 game with a solo home run.

Following Pettitte's seven-strikeout effort, Joba Chamberlain set down the Phillies in the seventh inning and Damaso Marte hurled a perfect eighth. After Phil Hughes surrendered a one-out homer to Ruiz in the bottom of the ninth, Girardi turned to Mariano Rivera to close things out.

"We feel good being up 2-1," Pettitte said. "But we know there's a lot of work left to do."

**WORLD SERIES 2009** · GAME 3

| N.Y. YANKEES | AB | R | H | RBI | BB | SO | LOB | AVG |
|---|---|---|---|---|---|---|---|---|
| Jeter, SS | 5 | 1 | 1 | 0 | 0 | 1 | 0 | .385 |
| Damon, LF | 4 | 1 | 1 | 2 | 1 | 0 | 0 | .167 |
| Teixeira, 1B | 3 | 1 | 0 | 0 | 2 | 2 | 1 | .100 |
| Rodriguez, 3B | 2 | 1 | 1 | 2 | 1 | 0 | 2 | .100 |
| Posada, C | 5 | 0 | 1 | 1 | 0 | 0 | 4 | .300 |
| Cano, 2B | 4 | 0 | 0 | 0 | 0 | 2 | 3 | .091 |
| Swisher, RF | 4 | 2 | 2 | 1 | 0 | 0 | 1 | .286 |
| Gardner, CF | 0 | 0 | 0 | 0 | 0 | 0 | 0 | .000 |
| Cabrera, CF-RF | 4 | 0 | 0 | 0 | 0 | 2 | 1 | .100 |
| Pettitte, P | 3 | 1 | 1 | 1 | 0 | 1 | 0 | .333 |
| Chamberlain, P | 0 | 0 | 0 | 0 | 0 | 0 | 0 | .000 |
| Matsui, PH | 1 | 1 | 1 | 1 | 0 | 0 | 0 | .571 |
| Marte, P | 0 | 0 | 0 | 0 | 0 | 0 | 0 | .000 |
| Hughes, P | 0 | 0 | 0 | 0 | 0 | 0 | 0 | .000 |
| Rivera, P | 0 | 0 | 0 | 0 | 0 | 0 | 0 | .000 |
| TOTALS | 35 | 8 | 8 | 8 | 4 | 8 | 12 | |

**BATTING:**

2B: Damon (1, Hamels); Swisher (1, Hamels). HR: Rodriguez (1, 4th inning off Hamels, 1 on, 1 out); Swisher (1, 6th inning off Happ, 0 on, 1 out); Matsui (2, 8th inning off Myers, 0 on, 2 out). TB: Jeter; Damon 2; Rodriguez 4; Posada; Swisher 6; Pettitte; Matsui 4. RBI: Damon (2); Rodriguez 2 (2); Posada (2); Swisher (1); Pettitte (1); Matsui (2). 2-out RBI: Posada; Matsui. Runners left in scoring position, 2 out: Posada; Cano. Team LOB: 6.

**BASERUNNING:**

SB: Damon (1, 2nd base off Durbin/Ruiz).

**FIELDING:**

E: Rodriguez (1, throw).

NEW YORK YANKEES    8
PHILADELPHIA PHILLIES    5

| | 1 | 2 | 3 | 4 | 5 | 6 | 7 | 8 | 9 | R | H | E |
|---|---|---|---|---|---|---|---|---|---|---|---|---|
| YANKEES | 0 | 0 | 0 | 2 | 3 | 1 | 1 | 1 | 0 | 8 | 8 | 1 |
| PHILLIES | 0 | 3 | 0 | 0 | 0 | 1 | 0 | 0 | 1 | 5 | 6 | 0 |

| PHILADELPHIA | AB | R | H | RBI | BB | SO | LOB | AVG |
|---|---|---|---|---|---|---|---|---|
| Rollins, SS | 4 | 0 | 1 | 1 | 1 | 0 | 1 | .200 |
| Victorino, CF | 3 | 0 | 0 | 1 | 0 | 0 | 1 | .182 |
| Utley, 2B | 4 | 0 | 0 | 0 | 0 | 2 | 3 | .182 |
| Howard, 1B | 4 | 0 | 0 | 0 | 0 | 3 | 1 | .154 |
| Werth, RF | 4 | 2 | 2 | 2 | 0 | 1 | 0 | .400 |
| Ibanez, LF | 4 | 0 | 0 | 0 | 0 | 2 | 0 | .250 |
| Feliz, 3B | 4 | 1 | 1 | 0 | 0 | 1 | 0 | .091 |
| Ruiz, C | 2 | 2 | 1 | 1 | 2 | 0 | 1 | .333 |
| Hamels, P | 1 | 0 | 1 | 0 | 0 | 0 | 0 | 1.000 |
| Happ, P | 0 | 0 | 0 | 0 | 0 | 0 | 0 | .000 |
| Bruntlett, PH | 1 | 0 | 0 | 0 | 0 | 0 | 1 | .000 |
| Durbin, P | 0 | 0 | 0 | 0 | 0 | 0 | 0 | .000 |
| Myers, P | 0 | 0 | 0 | 0 | 0 | 0 | 0 | .000 |
| Madson, P | 0 | 0 | 0 | 0 | 0 | 0 | 0 | .000 |
| Stairs, PH | 1 | 0 | 0 | 0 | 0 | 0 | 0 | .200 |
| TOTALS | 32 | 5 | 6 | 5 | 3 | 9 | 8 | |

**BATTING:**

2B: Feliz (1, Pettitte). HR: Werth 2 (2, 2nd inning off Pettitte, 0 on, 0 out; 6th inning off Pettitte, 0 on, 0 out); Ruiz (1, 9th inning off Hughes, 0 on, 1 out). TB: Rollins; Werth 8; Feliz 2; Ruiz 4; Hamels. RBI: Rollins (1); Victorino (2); Werth 2 (2); Ruiz (1). Runners left in scoring position, 2 out: Rollins, Utley, Howard. S: Hamels. SF: Victorino. Team LOB: 5.

**BASERUNNING:**

SB: Rollins (2, 2nd base off Pettitte/Posada)

| N.Y. YANKEES | IP | H | R | ER | BB | SO | HR | ERA |
|---|---|---|---|---|---|---|---|---|
| Pettitte (W, 1-0) | 6 | 5 | 4 | 4 | 3 | 7 | 2 | 6.00 |
| Chamberlain (H, 1) | 1 | 0 | 0 | 0 | 0 | 0 | 0 | 0.00 |
| Marte | 1 | 0 | 0 | 0 | 0 | 2 | 0 | 0.00 |
| Hughes | ⅓ | 1 | 1 | 1 | 0 | 0 | 1 | 81.00 |
| Rivera | ⅔ | 0 | 0 | 0 | 0 | 0 | 0 | 0.00 |

| PHILADELPHIA | IP | H | R | ER | BB | SO | HR | ERA |
|---|---|---|---|---|---|---|---|---|
| Hamels (L, 0-1) | 4⅓ | 5 | 5 | 5 | 2 | 3 | 1 | 10.38 |
| Happ | 1⅔ | 1 | 1 | 1 | 0 | 1 | 1 | 5.40 |
| Durbin | 1 | 1 | 1 | 1 | 1 | 2 | 0 | 9.00 |
| Myers | 1 | 1 | 1 | 1 | 0 | 2 | 1 | 9.00 |
| Madson | 1 | 0 | 0 | 0 | 1 | 0 | 0 | 0.00 |

HBP: Rodriguez (by Hamels); Rodriguez (by Durbin).

Pitches-strikes: Pettitte 104-59; Chamberlain 9-5; Marte 15-13; Hughes 8-5; Rivera 5-4. Hamels 69-49; Happ 21-12; Durbin 29-15; Myers 18-12; Madson 22-11.

Ground outs-fly outs: Pettitte 3-8; Chamberlain 1-2; Marte 0-1; Hughes 1-0; Rivera 1-1. Hamels 6-4; Happ 1-3; Durbin 0-1; Myers 0-1; Madson 1-2.

Batters faced: Pettitte 27; Chamberlain 3; Marte 3; Hughes 2; Rivera 2. Hamels 21; Happ 6; Durbin 6; Myers 4; Madson 4.

Inherited runners-scored: Happ 2-0.

Umpires: HP: Brian Gorman. 1B: Mike Everitt. 2B: Dana DeMuth. 3B: Joe West. LF: Gerry Davis. RF: Jeff Nelson.

Weather: 70 degrees, cloudy. Wind: 17 mph. T: 3:25 (1:20 delay). Att: 46,061.

# ON THE BRINK

BY ALFRED SANTASIERE III

## NINTH-INNING RALLY PUTS YANKEES ONE WIN FROM TITLE

### YANKEES ⑦ PHILLIES ④

**W**ith Game 4 of the World Series tied in the top of the ninth inning, Johnny Damon lined a two-out single to left field.

As Phillies closer Brad Lidge threw his first pitch to the next batter, Mark Teixeira, Damon broke for second base. With the Phillies infield shifted to the right, Damon slid safely into second base, jumped to his feet and took off for third base.

Phillies third baseman Pedro Feliz, who fielded the throw in front of second base, chased after Damon, but he was unable to tag him. Lidge, who neglected to cover third base,  watched the Yankees left fielder swipe third base standing up.

"When I saw Feliz behind me, I thought, 'Man, I hope I'm the Johnny Damon of 21 years old and not the 35-year-old guy,'" Damon said.

After Lidge plunked Teixeira, Alex Rodriguez doubled to left field, scoring Damon and giving the Yankees a 5-4 lead.

"There's no question about it; I have never had a bigger hit in my life," A-Rod said.

Jorge Posada followed with a single that plated Teixeira and Rodriguez and helped secure the Yankees' 7-4 victory.

# TENACIOUS D

**J**ohnny Damon's ninth-inning double steal was the type of play that will live on forever in Yankees lore, but Damon's overall performance in Game 4 was more than a footnote.

The veteran left fielder set a personal World Series best with three hits, including a clutch ninth-inning single that set up the game-winning run.

With the game tied, 4-4, Damon faced Phillies closer Brad Lidge with two outs and no one on. After a first-pitch ball, Damon fouled off three straight sliders. Lidge's next two offerings missed the strike zone, and with the count full, the entire Citizens Bank Park crowd stood in anticipation.

Damon continued to battle, fouling off two straight 94-mph heaters to stay alive. On the ninth pitch of the at-bat, he sent a soft liner to left field that fell in for a base hit. The double steal happened on the next pitch, and Alex Rodriguez' double sent Damon home with the eventual winning run.

"The whole key of that inning was an unbelievable, tenacious at-bat by Johnny Damon," Rodriguez said. "The guy is just a great competitor."

— Nathan Maciborski

POSADA HELPED SECURE THE VICTORY WITH A TWO-OUT, TWO-RUN SINGLE TO GIVE THE YANKEES A 7-4 LEAD.

Mariano Rivera closed out the Phillies in the bottom of the ninth, extending the Yankees' Series lead to 3 games to 1.

CC Sabathia started the game on three days' rest and battled the Phillies for 6 2/3 innings, giving up three runs.

The Yankees wasted little time spotting Sabathia a lead.

In the top of the first, Derek Jeter led off with an infield single and Damon lined a double to the right-field gap, moving the Yankees captain to third base.

Phillies starter Joe Blanton recorded the first out of the night when Teixeira grounded out to first base, but Jeter scored on the play.

Blanton's next pitch hit Rodriguez in the upper back. The plunking marked the third time A-Rod was hit by a pitch in the World Series and led home plate umpire Mike Everitt to issue a warning to both benches.

With one out, Posada hit a sacrifice fly to left field that scored Damon and gave the Yankees a 2-0 lead.

In the bottom of the first, Shane Victorino and Chase Utley hit back-to-back, one-out doubles off Sabathia, narrowing the Yankees lead to 2-1.

After Sabathia retired the Phillies in order in the second and third innings, Ryan Howard collected a leadoff single in the fourth and stole second base. With two outs, Feliz singled to left field and Howard beat Damon's throw to the plate, tying the game at 2-2.

The Yankees regained the lead in the top of the fifth inning, when Jeter singled in Nick Swisher. One batter later, Damon hit a bloop single to right field that scored Melky Cabrera and gave the Yankees a 4-2 advantage.

Blanton held the Yankees scoreless in the sixth and was replaced on the mound by Chan Ho Park at the start of the seventh.

Sabathia recorded two quick outs in the bottom of the seventh and then gave up a solo home run to Chase Utley on his 107th pitch of the night. With the Yankees clinging to a 4-3 lead, manager Joe Girardi replaced Sabathia with Damaso Marte, who retired Howard for the third out.

After striking out the first two batters in the bottom of the eighth, Joba Chamberlain yielded a game-tying home run to Feliz. Chamberlain rebounded by striking out Carlos Ruiz to end the frame.

"This team is so resilient," Chamberlain said about the Yankees' go-ahead rally in the ninth. "I can't say enough about these guys for picking me up."

WORLD SERIES 20 09 GAME 4

| NEW YORK YANKEES | 7 |
| PHILADELPHIA PHILLIES | 4 |

|  | 1 2 3 4 5 6 7 8 9 | R | H | E |
|---|---|---|---|---|
| YANKEES | 2 0 0 0 2 0 0 0 3 | 7 | 9 | 1 |
| PHILLIES | 1 0 0 1 0 0 1 1 0 | 4 | 8 | 1 |

| N.Y. YANKEES | AB | R | H | RBI | BB | SO | LOB | AVG |
|---|---|---|---|---|---|---|---|---|
| Jeter, SS | 4 | 1 | 2 | 1 | 1 | 1 | 0 | .412 |
| Damon, LF | 5 | 2 | 3 | 1 | 0 | 1 | 1 | .294 |
| Teixeira, 1B | 4 | 1 | 0 | 1 | 0 | 1 | 4 | .071 |
| Rodriguez, 3B | 4 | 1 | 1 | 1 | 0 | 1 | 2 | .143 |
| Posada, C | 3 | 0 | 1 | 3 | 1 | 2 | 0 | .308 |
| Cano, 2B | 4 | 0 | 1 | 0 | 0 | 1 | 1 | .133 |
| Swisher, RF | 2 | 1 | 0 | 0 | 2 | 2 | 2 | .222 |
| Cabrera, CF | 3 | 1 | 1 | 0 | 0 | 0 | 1 | .154 |
| Gardner, CF | 1 | 0 | 0 | 0 | 0 | 0 | 2 | .000 |
| Sabathia, P | 3 | 0 | 0 | 0 | 0 | 2 | 2 | .000 |
| Marte, P | 0 | 0 | 0 | 0 | 0 | 0 | 0 | .000 |
| Chamberlain, P | 0 | 0 | 0 | 0 | 0 | 0 | 0 | .000 |
| Matsui, PH | 1 | 0 | 0 | 0 | 0 | 0 | 0 | .500 |
| Rivera, P | 0 | 0 | 0 | 0 | 0 | 0 | 0 | .000 |
| TOTALS | 34 | 7 | 9 | 7 | 4 | 11 | 15 |  |

BATTING:

2B: Damon (2, Blanton); Rodriguez (1, Lidge). TB: Jeter 2; Damon 4; Rodriguez 2; Posada; Cano; Cabrera. RBI: Jeter (1); Damon (3); Teixeira (2); Rodriguez (3); Posada 3 (5). 2-out RBI: Rodriguez; Posada 2. Runners left in scoring position, 2 out: Rodriguez; Cano; Gardner. Team LOB: 7.

BASERUNNING:

SB: Damon 2 (3, 2nd base off Lidge/Ruiz; 3rd base off Lidge/Ruiz).

FIELDING:

E: Posada (1, missed catch).

| PHILADELPHIA | AB | R | H | RBI | BB | SO | LOB | AVG |
|---|---|---|---|---|---|---|---|---|
| Rollins, SS | 5 | 0 | 1 | 0 | 0 | 0 | 0 | .200 |
| Victorino, CF | 4 | 1 | 1 | 0 | 1 | 0 | 0 | .200 |
| Utley, 2B | 4 | 1 | 2 | 2 | 0 | 0 | 2 | .267 |
| Howard, 1B | 4 | 1 | 1 | 0 | 0 | 1 | 3 | .176 |
| Werth, RF | 3 | 0 | 0 | 0 | 1 | 2 | 3 | .308 |
| Ibanez, LF | 4 | 0 | 0 | 0 | 0 | 3 | 3 | .188 |
| Feliz, 3B | 4 | 1 | 3 | 2 | 0 | 0 | 0 | .267 |
| Ruiz, C | 3 | 0 | 0 | 0 | 1 | 1 | 1 | .250 |
| Blanton, P | 2 | 0 | 0 | 0 | 0 | 2 | 2 | .000 |
| Francisco, PH | 1 | 0 | 0 | 0 | 0 | 0 | 1 | .000 |
| Park, P | 0 | 0 | 0 | 0 | 0 | 0 | 0 | .000 |
| Madson, P | 0 | 0 | 0 | 0 | 0 | 0 | 0 | .000 |
| Lidge, P | 0 | 0 | 0 | 0 | 0 | 0 | 0 | .000 |
| Stairs, PH | 1 | 0 | 0 | 0 | 0 | 0 | 0 | .167 |
| TOTALS | 35 | 4 | 8 | 4 | 3 | 9 | 15 | |

**BATTING:**

2B: Victorino (1, Sabathia); Utley (1, Sabathia). HR: Utley (3, 7th inning off Sabathia, 0 on, 2 out); Feliz (1, 8th inning off Chamberlain, 0 on, 2 out). TB: Rollins; Victorino 2; Utley 6; Howard; Feliz 6. RBI: Utley 2 (4); Feliz 2 (2). 2-out RBI: Utley; Feliz 2. Runners left in scoring position, 2 out: Werth; Ibanez; Blanton; Francisco. Team LOB: 7.

**BASERUNNING:**

SB: Howard (1, 2nd base off Sabathia/Posada).

**FIELDING:**

E: Ibanez (1, throw). Outfield assists: Ibanez (Posada at 2nd base).

| N.Y. YANKEES | IP | H | R | ER | BB | SO | HR | ERA |
|---|---|---|---|---|---|---|---|---|
| Sabathia | 6⅔ | 7 | 3 | 3 | 3 | 6 | 1 | 3.29 |
| Marte (H, 1) | ⅓ | 0 | 0 | 0 | 0 | 0 | 0 | 0.00 |
| Chamberlain (BS,1) (W, 1-0) | 1 | 1 | 1 | 1 | 0 | 3 | 1 | 4.50 |
| Rivera (S, 2) | 1 | 0 | 0 | 0 | 0 | 0 | 0 | 0.00 |

| PHILADELPHIA | IP | H | R | ER | BB | SO | HR | ERA |
|---|---|---|---|---|---|---|---|---|
| Blanton | 6 | 5 | 4 | 4 | 2 | 7 | 0 | 6.00 |
| Park | 1 | 0 | 0 | 0 | 1 | 1 | 0 | 0.00 |
| Madson | 1 | 1 | 0 | 0 | 1 | 2 | 0 | 0.00 |
| Lidge (L, 0-1) | 1 | 3 | 3 | 3 | 0 | 1 | 0 | 27.00 |

IBB: Werth (by Sabathia); Ruiz (by Sabathia).

HBP: Teixeira (by Lidge); Rodriguez (by Blanton).

Pitches-strikes: Sabathia 107-67; Marte 4-3; Chamberlain 19-12; Rivera 8-6. Blanton 94-58; Park 14-8; Madson 20-11; Lidge 30-19.

Ground outs-fly outs: Sabathia 5-9; Marte 0-1; Chamberlain 0-0; Rivera 2-1. Blanton 4-7; Park 1-1; Madson 0-1; Lidge 0-1.

Batters faced: Sabathia 30; Marte 1; Chamberlain 4; Rivera 3. Blanton 26; Park 4; Madson 5; Lidge 6.

Umpires: HP: Mike Everitt. 1B: Dana DeMuth. 2B: Joe West. 3B: Gerry Davis. LF: Jeff Nelson. RF: Brian Gorman.

Weather: 49 degrees, cloudy. Wind: 3 mph. T: 3:25. Att: 46,145.

# EMPIRE STATE
# OF MIND

BY KEN DERRY

### PHILS BEAT YANKS TO SEND SERIES
### BACK TO NEW YORK

YANKEES  6 PHILLIES  8

**P**lastic sheets were rolled above the lockers in the visitors' clubhouse at Citizens Bank Park, but the Phillies put a cork in the Yankees' celebration plans and won Game 5 of the World Series, extending their season and sending the Series back to the Bronx.

The Phillies were aggressive and efficient, jumping on A.J. Burnett and making their hits count. Burnett left the game in the third inning without recording an out, having given up four hits and six runs in an eventual 8-6 loss.

The Yankees took a one-run lead in the first, when Johnny Damon scored on an Alex Rodriguez double off of lefthander Cliff Lee. But it only took three batters for Burnett to relinquish the lead.

Jimmy Rollins singled and moved to second after Burnett drilled Shane Victorino with a fastball on the hands. Chase Utley followed with a homer, and the Phils were on top, 3-1.

In the third, Burnett allowed the first four batters to reach base. He walked Utley and

Ryan Howard. Jayson Werth singled, scoring Utley, and Raul Ibanez scored Howard with another single. Ibanez was the last batter Burnett faced, his night ending after 53 pitches — 28 for strikes — and two-plus innings of work.

David Robertson, Burnett's replacement, allowed Werth to score — the sixth and final earned run charged to Burnett.

"I had a chance to do something special tonight, and I failed," Burnett said. "I let all the guys in here down, and I let a whole city down. These guys played their hearts out for all nine innings, but I didn't give us a chance to win."

With the score 6-1, Lee didn't look as sharp as his performance in Game 1, but he was sharp enough. After facing six batters in the first inning, he faced three in the second and fourth and didn't get into trouble again until the fifth. With one out, Lee walked Eric Hinske, who went to third on a single by Derek Jeter and scored on a grounder to first by Damon.

In the bottom of the seventh, Utley led off against lefthander Phil Coke and homered for the second time in the game and fifth in the World Series, tying Reggie Jackson's 1977 World Series record.

Ibanez homered three batters later, and with the score at 8-2, the Philadelphia fans seemed to take the fight out of the Yankees.

But the Bombers made it interesting in their final two frames.

In the top of the eighth, Damon and Mark Teixeira scored on a double off the bat of

Teixeira

# IT'S A SERIES
## OF SERIES FOR ERIC HINSKE

**E**ric Hinske was at it again. When the utilityman entered Game 5 in the top of the fifth inning as a pinch-hitter, he became just the second player to appear in three consecutive World Series with three different teams.

"My friends will text me and be like, 'Wow, you're the lucky charm. Every team you go to, you go to the World Series,'" Hinske told The Post-Crescent, a newspaper in his home state of Wisconsin. "It never gets old. You don't get used to it. I've been lucky, man. I've been real lucky."

Hinske appeared as a pinch-hitter in Game 1 of the 2007 World Series with the Red Sox and in Games 4 and 5 of the 2008 Fall Classic with the Rays. In Game 4 of the latter Series, Hinske took Philadelphia starter Joe Blanton deep in an eventual 10-2 Rays loss.

According to the Elias Sports Bureau, Hinske joined Don Baylor in accomplishing the feat. Baylor went to the World Series with Boston in 1986, Minnesota in 1987 and Oakland in 1988.

— Kristina M. Dodge

LEE WON HIS SECOND
GAME OF THE SERIES
TO SEND IT BACK TO
NEW YORK.

Rodriguez, his second of the night and third RBI of the game. Then with one out, A-Rod scored on a Robinson Cano sacrifice fly to make it 8-5.

In the top of the ninth, Jorge Posada greeted new pitcher Ryan Madson with a leadoff double and moved to third on a pinch-hit single by Hideki Matsui. Jeter followed by grounding into a double play, but Posada scored, making it 8-6, and Damon continued the rally with a single to center. Up stepped Teixeira, batting from the left side and representing the tying run. But Madson went ahead, 1-2, and got Teixeira to fish for a changeup, striking out to end the rally and the game.

It would be a New York celebration for certain. The only thing left to decide was the champion.

*Jeter*

WORLD SERIES
20 09
*Fall Classic*

GAME 5

**NEW YORK YANKEES** 6
**PHILADELPHIA PHILLIES** 8

| | 1 2 3 4 5 6 7 8 9 | R | H | E |
|---|---|---|---|---|
| YANKEES | 1 0 0 0 1 0 0 3 1 | 6 | 10 | 0 |
| PHILLIES | 3 0 3 0 0 0 2 0 X | 8 | 9 | 0 |

| N.Y. YANKEES | AB | R | H | RBI | BB | SO | LOB | AVG |
|---|---|---|---|---|---|---|---|---|
| Jeter, SS | 5 | 0 | 1 | 0 | 0 | 0 | 1 | .364 |
| Damon, LF | 4 | 2 | 3 | 1 | 1 | 0 | 1 | .381 |
| Teixeira, 1B | 5 | 1 | 1 | 0 | 0 | 1 | 4 | .105 |
| Rodriguez, 3B | 4 | 1 | 2 | 3 | 0 | 0 | 1 | .222 |
| Swisher, RF | 3 | 0 | 0 | 0 | 1 | 0 | 1 | .167 |
| Cano, 2B | 3 | 0 | 1 | 1 | 0 | 2 | | .167 |
| Gardner, CF | 4 | 0 | 0 | 0 | 0 | 1 | 1 | .000 |
| Molina, C | 1 | 0 | 0 | 0 | 0 | 0 | 0 | .000 |
| Posada, PH-C | 3 | 1 | 1 | 0 | 0 | 1 | 0 | .313 |
| Burnett, P | 1 | 0 | 0 | 0 | 0 | 1 | 0 | .000 |
| Robertson, P | 0 | 0 | 0 | 0 | 0 | 0 | 0 | .000 |
| Hinske, PH | 0 | 1 | 0 | 0 | 1 | 0 | 0 | .000 |
| Aceves, P | 0 | 0 | 0 | 0 | 0 | 0 | 0 | .000 |
| Hairston, PH | 1 | 0 | 0 | 0 | 0 | 0 | 0 | .250 |
| Coke, P | 0 | 0 | 0 | 0 | 0 | 0 | 0 | .000 |
| Hughes, P | 0 | 0 | 0 | 0 | 0 | 0 | 0 | .000 |
| Matsui-PH | 1 | 0 | 1 | 0 | 0 | 0 | 0 | .556 |
| TOTALS | 35 | 6 | 10 | 5 | 3 | 4 | 11 | |

BATTING:

2B: Teixeira (1, Lee); Rodriguez 2 (3, Lee, Lee); Posada (1, Madson). TB: Jeter; Damon 3; Teixeira 2; Rodriguez 4; Cano; Posada 2; Matsui. RBI: Damon (4); Rodriguez 3 (6); Cano (1). 2-out RBI: Rodriguez. Runners left in scoring position, 2 out: Teixeira 2; Cano. SF: Cano. GIDP: Jeter. Team LOB: 6.

FIELDING:

DP: (Cano-Jeter-Teixeira).

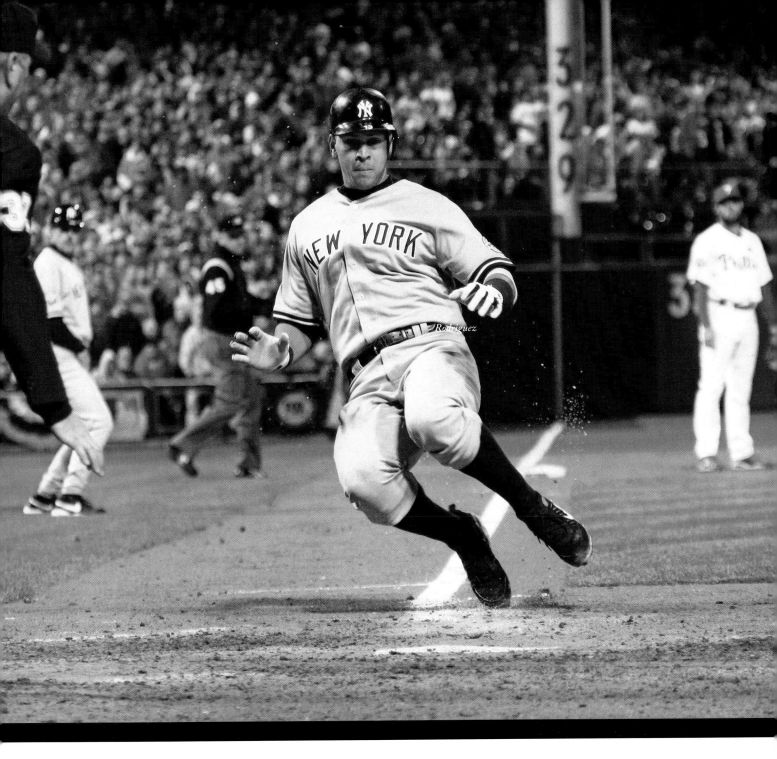

| PHILADELPHIA | AB | R | H | RBI | BB | SO | LOB | AVG |
|---|---|---|---|---|---|---|---|---|
| Rollins, SS | 4 | 1 | 2 | 0 | 1 | 1 | 2 | .263 |
| Victorino, CF | 3 | 1 | 0 | 0 | 0 | 0 | 2 | .167 |
| Francisco, CF | 0 | 0 | 0 | 0 | 1 | 0 | 0 | .000 |
| Utley, 2B | 3 | 3 | 2 | 4 | 2 | 0 | 0 | .333 |
| Howard, 1B | 2 | 1 | 0 | 0 | 0 | 2 | 0 | .158 |
| Werth, RF | 4 | 1 | 1 | 1 | 0 | 1 | 1 | .294 |
| Ibanez, LF | 4 | 1 | 2 | 2 | 0 | 0 | 1 | .250 |
| Feliz, 3B | 4 | 0 | 0 | 0 | 0 | 1 | 3 | .211 |
| Ruiz, C | 4 | 0 | 1 | 1 | 0 | 1 | 1 | .250 |
| Lee, P | 3 | 0 | 1 | 0 | 0 | 1 | 0 | .333 |
| Park, P | 0 | 0 | 0 | 0 | 0 | 0 | 0 | .000 |
| Stairs, PH | 1 | 0 | 0 | 0 | 0 | 0 | 1 | .143 |
| Madson, P | 0 | 0 | 0 | 0 | 0 | 0 | 0 | .000 |
| TOTALS | 32 | 8 | 9 | 8 | 4 | 7 | 11 | |

**BATTING:**

HR: Utley 2 (5, 1st inning off Burnett, 2 on, 0 out; 7th inning off Coke, 0 on, 0 out); Ibanez (1, 7th inning off Coke, 0 on, 2 out). TB: Rollins 2; Utley 8; Werth; Ibanez 5; Ruiz; Lee. RBI: Utley 4 (8); Werth (3); Ibanez 2 (4); Ruiz (2). 2-out RBI: Ibanez. Runners left in scoring position, 2 out: Rollins; Victorino. GIDP: Stairs. Team LOB: 5.

**BASERUNNING:**

SB: Utley (1, 2nd base off Burnett/Molina).

**FIELDING:**

DP: (Rollins-Utley-Howard).

| N.Y. YANKEES | IP | H | R | ER | BB | SO | HR | ERA |
|---|---|---|---|---|---|---|---|---|
| Burnett (L, 1-1) | 2 | 4 | 6 | 6 | 4 | 2 | 1 | 7.00 |
| Robertson | 2 | 1 | 0 | 0 | 0 | 2 | 0 | 0.00 |
| Aceves | 2 | 1 | 0 | 0 | 0 | 1 | 0 | 0.00 |
| Coke | ⅔ | 2 | 2 | 2 | 0 | 1 | 2 | 13.50 |
| Hughes | 1⅓ | 1 | 0 | 0 | 0 | 1 | 0 | 16.20 |

| PHILADELPHIA | IP | H | R | ER | BB | SO | HR | ERA |
|---|---|---|---|---|---|---|---|---|
| Lee (W, 2-0) | 7 | 7 | 5 | 5 | 3 | 3 | 0 | 2.81 |
| Park | 1 | 0 | 0 | 0 | 0 | 0 | 0 | 0.00 |
| Madson (S, 1) | 1 | 3 | 1 | 1 | 0 | 1 | 0 | 2.25 |

Burnett pitched to four batters in the 3rd.

Lee pitched to three batters in the 8th.

WP: Aceves  HBP: Victorino (by Burnett).

Pitches-strikes: Burnett 53-28; Robertson 27-17; Aceves 19-14; Coke 19-11; Hughes 12-10. Lee 112-70; Park 11-7; Madson 24-14.

Ground outs-fly outs: Burnett 3-1; Robertson 3-1; Aceves 3-2; Coke 0-1; Hughes 3-0. Lee 9-9; Park 1-2; Madson 2-0.

Batters faced: Burnett 15; Robertson 7; Aceves 7; Coke 4; Hughes 4. Lee 31; Park 3; Madson 5.

Inherited runners-scored: Robertson 2-1. Park 1-1.

Umpires: HP: Dana DeMuth. 1B: Joe West. 2B: Gerry Davis. 3B: Jeff Nelson. LF: Brian Gorman. RF: Mike Everitt.

Weather: 50 degrees, cloudy. Wind: 5 mph. T: 3:26. Att: 46,178.

# BACK ON TOP

BY CRAIG TAPPER

## YANKEES CAPTURE NO. 27

PHILLIES  YANKEES

For the 27th time, the New York Yankees earned their place as the top team in baseball. With a barrage of RBI hits from Hideki Matsui and another clutch outing from Andy Pettitte, the Yankees defeated the Phillies, 7-3, to close out the Fall Classic in six games and capture the franchise's first world championship since 2000.

"This is what the Steinbrenner family has strived for year after year after year and has tried to deliver to the city of New York," said Yankees manager Joe Girardi. "George Steinbrenner and his family are champions. To be able to deliver this to the Boss, the Stadium that he created and the atmosphere he has created around here is very gratifying for all of us."

Matsui began the scoring in the second inning, when he swatted a two-run home run off Phillies starter Pedro Martinez on the eighth pitch of the at-bat. It was Matsui's third home run of the Series.

"Tonight, [Matsui] was huge," Girardi said. "I just think about the first at-bat that he had against Pedro, what a tough at-bat, and he hit some balls hard foul and he kept at it and kept at it and got us the lead, and I thought that was extremely important."

After the Phillies cut the lead in half on a Jimmy Rollins sacrifice fly in the top of the third, Matsui came through again in the bottom of the inning. On an 0-2 pitch with two outs, Matsui sliced a two-run single to center, plating Derek Jeter and Johnny Damon to extend the Yankees' lead to 4-1. Mark Teixeira's fifth-inning RBI single added to the lead, and Matsui capped his night with a two-run double in the same frame, giving the Yankees a 7-1 cushion and easing the tensions of a potentially stressful game.

Pitching on short rest for the first time since Sept. 30, 2006, Pettitte hurled 5 ⅔ innings of three-run ball. He became just the second Yankees pitcher to finish a single postseason with a 4-0 record.

"My command wasn't real good, but I was able to get through it and make some pitches when I had to," Pettitte said. "I'm just very thankful for that."

Pettitte worked out of jams with double plays in the first and fifth innings and induced an inning-ending grounder with runners on first and second in the fourth frame. His lone costly mistake was a first-pitch slider that Ryan Howard took the opposite way for a home run with one out in the sixth.

Joba Chamberlain relieved Pettitte, worked out of the sixth inning and got the first two outs of the seventh before handing the ball off to Damaso Marte. The lefty struck out Chase

Utley to end the inning and began the eighth inning by fanning Howard.

Girardi then turned the ball over to Mariano Rivera. Staked to a 7-3 lead, the final five outs felt like a given.

"It's over," Jeter said, when describing his feelings with Rivera on the mound in that situation. "That's what's in everybody's minds. He's human; he's going to give up some runs here and there. But a four-run lead? We could have gone and played another nine innings [with that lead]."

MARTINEZ LASTED
JUST FOUR INNINGS,
ALLOWING THREE HITS,
TWO WALKS AND
FOUR RUNS.

With two outs in the top of the ninth inning, Robinson Cano fielded a routine grounder off the bat of Shane Victorino and tossed the ball to Teixeira at first for the final out of the 2009 season.

Said Yankees president Randy Levine, "The Yankees won. The world is right again."

# MATSUI NAMED WORLD SERIES MVP

**H**ideki Matsui had been clutch all Series long, but it was his record-tying, six-RBI performance in Game 6 that secured him top honors: World Series Most Valuable Player.

Matsui tagged Phillies righthander Pedro Martinez for a second-inning, two-run homer and added to his RBI total in the third with a two-run single. He knocked in Nos. 5 and 6 in the fifth off reliever J.A. Happ, tying former Yankees second baseman Bobby Richardson's single-game World Series record, set in Game 3 of the 1960 Classic.

"They're partying in Tokyo tonight," said Nick Swisher. "I know that. What a great job Matsui did for us, coming up in clutch situations all year long. He deserved that MVP trophy, no doubt about it."

Matsui finished the World Series 8-for-13 (.615) with three home runs, three runs scored and eight RBI. His 1.385 slugging percentage was second only to Lou Gehrig's 1.727 mark set during the Yanks' 1928 sweep of the Cardinals.

The designated hitter became the first Japanese player to win the award and the first player to win it without playing a single inning in the field.

"I guess you could say this is the best moment of my life right now," Matsui said.

**— Kristina M. Dodge**

# FOR THE BOSS

**O**nce the final out of the World Series had been recorded, the Yankees went from exuberantly piling on top of each other to reflecting on their incredible journey together.

On a stage set up near second base, the team accepted trophies and shared a few words with the crowd. At the forefront of everyone's thoughts was the message displayed on the centerfield video board: "Boss, This Is For You."

The Yankees' principal owner since 1973, George Steinbrenner was the driving force behind the team's 2009 world championship — the seventh under his watch — as well as the sparkling new Yankee Stadium in the Bronx. Although he watched the team clinch its 27th title from his home in Florida, Steinbrenner's presence was felt.

"He's certainly here in spirit," said Yankees managing general partner/co-chairperson Hal Steinbrenner. "This whole thing was all about my father. This one is for him."

"We all wanted to win it for him," said team captain Derek Jeter.

Steinbrenner released a statement that read in part: "Every World Series victory is special, but this one is especially sweet coming in the first year in our new home. We are so grateful to our fans. This World Series belongs to them and to all Yankees — past, present and future."

— Nathan Maciborski

---

WORLD SERIES 2009

GAME 6

| PHILADELPHIA | AB | R | H | RBI | BB | SO | LOB | AVG |
|---|---|---|---|---|---|---|---|---|
| Rollins, SS | 4 | 0 | 0 | 1 | 0 | 0 | 3 | .217 |
| Victorino, CF | 4 | 0 | 1 | 0 | 1 | 0 | 1 | .182 |
| Utley, 2B | 3 | 1 | 0 | 0 | 1 | 2 | 3 | .286 |
| Howard, 1B | 4 | 1 | 1 | 2 | 0 | 1 | 0 | .174 |
| Werth, RF | 2 | 0 | 0 | 0 | 2 | 2 | 0 | .263 |
| Ibanez, DH | 3 | 0 | 2 | 0 | 1 | 0 | 1 | .304 |
| Feliz, 3B | 4 | 0 | 0 | 0 | 0 | 0 | 5 | .174 |
| Francisco, LF | 3 | 0 | 0 | 0 | 0 | 2 | 0 | .000 |
| Stairs, PH | 1 | 0 | 0 | 0 | 0 | 0 | 0 | .125 |
| Ruiz, C | 2 | 1 | 2 | 0 | 2 | 0 | 0 | .333 |
| TOTALS | 30 | 3 | 6 | 3 | 7 | 7 | 13 | |

| | | |
|---|---|---|
| PHILADELPHIA PHILLIES | | 3 |
| NEW YORK YANKEES | | 7 |

| | 1 | 2 | 3 | 4 | 5 | 6 | 7 | 8 | 9 | | R | H | E |
|---|---|---|---|---|---|---|---|---|---|---|---|---|---|
| PHILLIES | 0 | 0 | 1 | 0 | 0 | 2 | 0 | 0 | 0 | | 3 | 6 | 0 |
| YANKEES | 0 | 2 | 2 | 0 | 3 | 0 | 0 | 0 | X | | 7 | 8 | 0 |

**BATTING:**
2B: Ibanez 2 (4, Pettitte, Rivera). 3B: Ruiz (1, Pettitte). HR: Howard (1, 6th inning off Pettitte, 1 on, 1 out). TB: Victorino; Howard 4; Ibanez 4; Ruiz 4. RBI: Rollins (2); Howard 2 (3). Runners left in scoring position, 2 out: Victorino; Utley; Feliz 4. SF: Rollins. GIDP: Rollins; Utley. Team LOB: 8.

**BASERUNNING:**
SB: Rollins (3, 2nd base off Chamberlain/Posada).

| N.Y. YANKEES | AB | R | H | RBI | BB | SO | LOB | AVG |
|---|---|---|---|---|---|---|---|---|
| Jeter, SS | 5 | 2 | 3 | 0 | 0 | 0 | 1 | .407 |
| Damon, LF | 1 | 1 | 0 | 0 | 1 | 1 | 0 | .364 |
| Hairston, LF | 2 | 0 | 0 | 0 | 0 | 0 | 2 | .167 |
| Teixeira, 1B | 3 | 1 | 1 | 1 | 1 | 0 | 1 | .136 |
| Rodriguez, 3B | 2 | 2 | 1 | 0 | 2 | 1 | 3 | .250 |
| Matsui, DH | 4 | 1 | 3 | 6 | 0 | 1 | 1 | .615 |
| Posada, C | 3 | 0 | 0 | 0 | 1 | 2 | 3 | .263 |
| Cano, 2B | 4 | 0 | 0 | 0 | 0 | 2 | 3 | .136 |
| Swisher, RF | 3 | 0 | 0 | 0 | 1 | 1 | 0 | .133 |
| Gardner, CF | 4 | 0 | 0 | 0 | 0 | 2 | 1 | .000 |
| TOTALS | 31 | 7 | 8 | 7 | 5 | 11 | 14 | |

**BATTING:**

2B: Jeter (3, Durbin); Matsui (1, Happ). HR: Matsui (3, 2nd inning off Martinez, 1 on, 0 out). TB: Jeter 4; Teixeira; Rodriguez; Matsui 7. RBI: Teixeira (3); Matsui 6 (8). 2-out RBI: Matsui 2. Runners left in scoring position, 2 out: Posada; Cano 2. S: Hairston. Team LOB: 7.

**BASERUNNING:**

SB: Rodriguez (1, 2nd base off Eyre/Ruiz).

**FIELDING:**

PB: Posada (1). DP: 2 (Cano-Jeter-Teixeira; Rodriguez-Cano-Teixeira).

| PHILADELPHIA | IP | H | R | ER | BB | SO | HR | ERA |
|---|---|---|---|---|---|---|---|---|
| Martinez (L, 0-2) | 4 | 3 | 4 | 4 | 2 | 5 | 1 | 6.30 |
| Durbin | ⅓ | 2 | 3 | 3 | 1 | 0 | 0 | 27.00 |
| Happ | 1 | 1 | 0 | 0 | 1 | 3 | 0 | 3.38 |
| Park | 1 | 1 | 0 | 0 | 0 | 1 | 0 | 0.00 |
| Eyre | 1⅓ | 0 | 0 | 0 | 1 | 2 | 0 | 0.00 |
| Madson | ⅓ | 1 | 0 | 0 | 0 | 0 | 0 | 2.08 |

| N.Y. YANKEES | IP | H | R | ER | BB | SO | HR | ERA |
|---|---|---|---|---|---|---|---|---|
| Pettitte (W, 2-0) | 5⅔ | 4 | 3 | 3 | 5 | 3 | 1 | 5.40 |
| Chamberlain | 1 | 1 | 0 | 0 | 1 | 1 | 0 | 3.00 |
| Marte (H, 2) | ⅔ | 0 | 0 | 0 | 0 | 2 | 0 | 0.00 |
| Rivera | 1⅔ | 1 | 0 | 0 | 1 | 1 | 0 | 0.00 |

WP: Pettitte.

IBB: Posada (by Eyre). HBP: Teixeira (by Martinez).

Pitches-strikes: Martinez 77-46; Durbin 15-7; Happ 28-15; Park 17-11; Eyre 21-10; Madson 4-3. Pettitte 94-50; Chamberlain 21-11; Marte 6-6; Rivera 41-26.

Ground outs-fly outs:  Martinez 0-7; Durbin 1-0; Happ 0-0; Park 1-1; Eyre 2-0; Madson 0-1. Pettitte 9-5; Chamberlain 2-0; Marte 0-0; Rivera 1-3.

Batters faced: Martinez 18; Durbin 4; Happ 5; Park 4; Eyre 5; Madson 2. Pettitte 24; Chamberlain 5; Marte 2; Rivera 7.

Inherited runners-scored: Happ 2-2; Park 1-0; Eyre 1-0. Chamberlain 1-0; Marte 2-0.

Umpires:  HP: Joe West. 1B: Gerry Davis. 2B: Jeff Nelson. 3B: Brian Gorman. LF: Mike Everitt. RF: Dana DeMuth.

Weather: 47 degrees, cloudy. Wind: 7 mph. T: 3:52. Att: 50,315.

# HIDEKI MATSUI

BY BOB KLAPISCH

Hideki Matsui held the World Series MVP trophy high over his head on a cool November night — the greatest of his professional career — for the world to see. The Japanese slugger then peered out at his teammates in front of him and broke into laughter as they started chanting for his interpreter, Roger Kahlon, who joined Matsui on stage.

What wasn't there to smile about after single-handedly conquering the Phillies in Game 6 of the World Series, driving in six runs and being voted the Fall Classic's Most Valuable Player?

No Japanese player had ever won the prestigious award. No player besides former Yankees second baseman Bobby Richardson in 1960 had totaled that many RBI in a Series game. No Bomber had changed the balance of power against the Phillies as dramatically as Matsui. No one could stop him.

"He hit everything we threw up there," said Philadelphia manager Charlie Manuel. "It wasn't just our righties, but he squared up on our lefties, too. He's a pretty good hitter."

There are countless ways to remember Matsui's contributions in the Series — he hit .615 with three homers and eight RBI —

but his signature at-bat came against Pedro Martinez in the second inning of Game 6. He smashed a two-run home run that gave the Yankees a lead they never relinquished.

Martinez, who had surrendered a home run to Matsui on a curveball in Game 2, attacked the designated hitter with only fastballs in their rematch. But that plan failed, too, as Matsui sent a middle-of-the-plate offering into the middle deck in right field.

Naturally, the Yankee Stadium crowd went berserk as Martinez lowered his head in regret. But Matsui didn't gloat; he was never wired for that. Instead, he circled the bases quickly and respectfully and waited until he was in the dugout to begin exchanging high fives.

That's Matsui, the most self-contained man in the clubhouse.

"Hideki is as quiet a superstar as I've

ever seen anywhere," Bernie Williams once said. "He's representing the whole Japanese culture here. It's a lot of weight on his shoulders, and yet he doesn't get rattled."

Not even the uncertainty of his future seemed to upset Matsui, who was preparing to declare free agency during the offseason. While the Yankees were deeply appreciative of Matsui's seven years in New York, no one could guarantee there would be a spot on the 2010 roster for a 35-year-old designated hitter with bad knees.

No matter, said Matsui, who told the crowd — and the world — "I love New York. I love the Yankees. I love the fans here. I hope everything works out well. I'm just happy right now."

He didn't have to ask if the feeling was mutual. The cheering crowd delivered that verdict loud and clear.

## 2009 NEW YORK YANKEES · POSTSEASON STATISTICS

| Pitching | W-L | ERA | G | GS | SV | IP | H | R | BB | SO |
|---|---|---|---|---|---|---|---|---|---|---|
| Aceves, Alfredo | 0-1 | 4.15 | 4 | 0 | 0 | 4 $\frac{1}{3}$ | 5 | 2 | 3 | 2 |
| Bruney, Brian | 0-0 | 54.00 | 1 | 0 | 0 | $\frac{1}{3}$ | 3 | 2 | 0 | 0 |
| Burnett, A.J. | 1-1 | 5.27 | 5 | 5 | 0 | 27 $\frac{1}{3}$ | 22 | 16 | 16 | 24 |
| Chamberlain, Joba | 1-0 | 2.84 | 10 | 0 | 0 | 6 $\frac{1}{3}$ | 9 | 2 | 1 | 7 |
| Coke, Phil | 0-0 | 6.75 | 6 | 0 | 0 | 2 $\frac{2}{3}$ | 4 | 2 | 1 | 3 |
| Gaudin, Chad | 0-0 | 0.00 | 1 | 0 | 0 | 1 | 0 | 0 | 0 | 0 |
| Hughes, Phil | 0-1 | 8.53 | 9 | 0 | 0 | 6 $\frac{1}{3}$ | 11 | 6 | 4 | 7 |
| Marte, Damaso | 0-0 | 0.00 | 8 | 0 | 0 | 4 | 2 | 0 | 0 | 5 |
| Pettitte, Andy | 4-0 | 3.52 | 5 | 5 | 0 | 30 $\frac{2}{3}$ | 26 | 12 | 11 | 25 |
| Rivera, Mariano | 0-0 | 0.56 | 12 | 0 | 5 | 16 | 10 | 1 | 5 | 14 |
| Robertson, David | 2-0 | 0.00 | 5 | 0 | 0 | 5 $\frac{1}{3}$ | 4 | 0 | 3 | 3 |
| Sabathia, CC | 3-1 | 1.98 | 5 | 5 | 0 | 36 $\frac{1}{3}$ | 28 | 9 | 9 | 32 |

| Hitting | G | AB | R | H | 2B | 3B | HR | RBI | SB | AVG |
|---|---|---|---|---|---|---|---|---|---|---|
| Burnett, A.J. | 1 | 1 | 0 | 0 | 0 | 0 | 0 | 0 | 0 | .000 |
| Cabrera, Melky | 13 | 48 | 5 | 13 | 2 | 0 | 0 | 4 | 0 | .271 |
| Cano, Robinson | 15 | 57 | 5 | 11 | 1 | 2 | 0 | 6 | 0 | .193 |
| Cervelli, Francisco | 2 | 1 | 0 | 0 | 0 | 0 | 0 | 0 | 0 | .000 |
| Damon, Johnny | 15 | 64 | 10 | 18 | 3 | 0 | 2 | 9 | 3 | .281 |
| Gardner, Brett | 14 | 13 | 3 | 2 | 0 | 0 | 0 | 0 | 1 | .154 |
| Guzman, Freddy | 2 | 1 | 0 | 0 | 0 | 0 | 0 | 0 | 0 | .000 |
| Hairston Jr., Jerry | 6 | 8 | 1 | 2 | 0 | 0 | 0 | 0 | 0 | .250 |
| Hinske, Eric | 1 | 0 | 1 | 0 | 0 | 0 | 0 | 0 | 0 | - |
| Jeter, Derek | 15 | 64 | 14 | 22 | 5 | 0 | 3 | 6 | 0 | .344 |
| Matsui, Hideki | 15 | 43 | 5 | 15 | 2 | 0 | 4 | 13 | 0 | .349 |
| Molina, Jose | 5 | 6 | 0 | 1 | 0 | 0 | 0 | 0 | 0 | .167 |
| Pettitte, Andy | 1 | 3 | 1 | 1 | 0 | 0 | 0 | 1 | 0 | .333 |
| Posada, Jorge | 15 | 50 | 5 | 13 | 2 | 0 | 2 | 8 | 1 | .260 |
| Rodriguez, Alex | 15 | 52 | 15 | 19 | 5 | 0 | 6 | 18 | 2 | .365 |
| Sabathia, CC | 1 | 3 | 0 | 0 | 0 | 0 | 0 | 0 | 0 | .000 |
| Swisher, Nick | 14 | 47 | 5 | 6 | 2 | 0 | 1 | 2 | 0 | .128 |
| Teixeira, Mark | 15 | 61 | 10 | 11 | 2 | 0 | 2 | 8 | 0 | .180 |

# MARCH OF THE CHAMPIONS

## HEROES AGAIN, THE YANKEES CELEBRATE A RETURN TO GLORY

BY KEN DERRY

There is thunder in the canyon.
Concussions pound like a ravaged heart,
sending a dysrhythmia of echoes from side
to side. Horns blow, their baritone notes
hanging in the sky, floating with the streams
of toilet paper above. More shreds of paper
fall to the ground like soft snow.

An army of millions spreads north. Maybe there are more. Maybe not. A head count is out of the question. Perhaps they arrived in the predawn dark and huddled to keep warm, saving their energy for the imminent spectacle. Perhaps more are on their way.

This is the way it is during the New York Yankees World Series parade up the Canyon of Heroes in Lower Manhattan on Nov. 6, 2009. And this is the way it has been at Broadway and Battery Place, where bloody conquests, raw deals and victorious celebrations have been marked by concussions of thunder for hundreds of years.

Before Broadway had the canyon, before it had the Great White Way, before it was a multilane thoroughfare stretching from Battery Park to Inwood, it was the Wickquasgeck Trail. Nothing more than a snaking dirt path, the trail was the main concourse up and down the island, used mostly by the Lenape Indians. When outside powers threatened the local livelihood, it was on this route that warriors marched to defend it.

Henry Hudson is credited with mapping the area beginning in 1609 on his voyage up the river that now bears his name. In 1626, the Dutch acquired what they had already been calling New Amsterdam from American Indians for goods worth about 60 guilders. Depending on the source, the pot is equal to anything between $24 and $1,000.

Just a few steps north of Broadway and Battery Place is Bowling Green, the oldest public park in New York City and the site where the transaction to acquire the island occurred.

Today, it's the last stop in Manhattan before entering Brooklyn on the Nos. 4 and 5 trains, which are running free during the parade. Bowling Green is also the point that Yankees stars CC Sabathia and Mark Teixeira emerge from a VIP area to board a parade float. Throngs of fans shout their names, and the pair seems to be absorbing all the attention.

26 BROADWAY

26 Broadway

So focused during the season, today, they are world champions, and they should absorb what is meant for them.

There is a lot to absorb in the Canyon of Heroes. There's the charging bull at the north end of Bowling Green. There's the Gothic architecture. There's the whipping November winds. There are endless rolls of toilet paper soaring from any of the million pairs of hands that have come to applaud the Yankees. Fans are shoulder to shoulder on the street; they've climbed trees; they're standing on narrow ledges outside office windows three stories high.

Wait, what's that climbing up the light post in Liberty Plaza on Cedar Street? Is that Big Bird?

"Who-Are-You!" the fans chant as Yankees employees riding in an NYC Ducks tour vehicle lurch past them.

Fans have come to see the players, and when the floats carrying Derek Jeter and Mariano Rivera and Andy Pettitte and Jorge Posada roll by, the Canyon of Heroes erupts into an open-air asylum, a veritable love-in for all things pinstriped.

"That was very cool," Teixeira says when the ride to City Hall is over. "You see 50,000 a night, and obviously they're into it, but to see millions of New Yorkers, it makes you

*Alex Rodriguez*

*Alex Rodriguez*

proud to play for such a great city."

The first New York City ticker-tape parade was an impromptu celebration in 1886 for the dedication of the Statue of Liberty. Ticker-tape parades were uncommon in the years that followed. They were reserved for special occasions, mostly for presidents, generals and kings. But even scientist Albert Einstein had his moment in 1921.

In 1924, U.S. Olympic athletes had their own parade. It paved the way for future sports figures and teams, among them Bobby Jones, the 1926 winner of the British Open golf tournament, and the New York Giants, baseball's winners of the National League pennant in 1954.

The Yankees have taken floats to City Hall nine times. The first was in 1961 for winning the American League pennant in 1960. Another trip followed in 1962 for the previous year's world championship. The Bombers didn't take another ride until they won the World Series in 1977 and again in '78. In 1996, the Yankees recaptured the world championship and returned to the Canyon of Heroes, followed by parades in 1998, '99 and 2000.

"You feel like the president," Jeter says after his fifth parade. "You could do this every day, and you wouldn't get tired of it."

*Teixeira*

*Jeter*

*Sabathia*

*Joe Girardi [L] and
New York City Mayor
Michael Bloomberg*

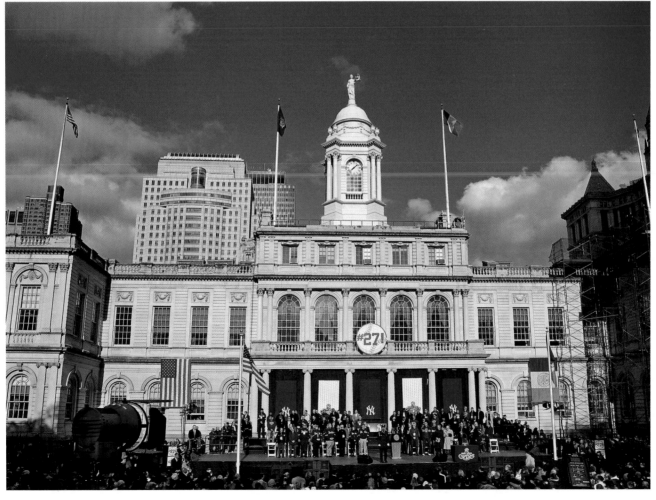

*Hideki Matsui*

Jorge Posada

Jeter

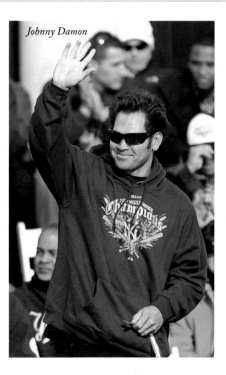

Johnny Damon

For all who are there, Yankees principal owner George Steinbrenner is not. He is remembered and missed.

"We wouldn't have this Stadium, we wouldn't have this team without him," Jeter says. "That's the bottom line. I'm glad we were able to win one for him."

A new boom echoes in the canyon. It's the sanitation department. The festivities at City Hall have yet to conclude. Dignitaries have spoken. The players have received their keys to the city. But rapper Jay-Z is

*Jay-Z*

"YOU FEEL LIKE THE PRESIDENT. YOU COULD DO THIS EVERY DAY, AND YOU WOULDN'T GET TIRED OF IT."

— JETER

mid verse in his ubiquitous hit "Empire State of Mind." That doesn't stop sanitation workers and volunteers. They are sweeping the streets clean, albeit with some hip-hop in their step. Brooms are pushed. Collection trucks are nearly full. Street cleaners are washing Broadway.

All in preparation for traffic. All in preparation for the next roll of thunder.